Closing
that Gift!

Closing that Gift!

How to be Successful 99% of the Time

Robert F. Hartsook, JD, EdD

author of How to Get Million Dollar Gifts
and Have Donors ThanK You!

First Printing: 1999
Second Printing: 1999
Third Printing: 2000

Additional copies of this book are available from the publisher. Discounts may apply to large-quantity orders.

Address all inquiries to:
ASR Philanthropic Publishing
P.O. Box 782648
Wichita, Kansas 67278
Telephone: 316.733.7470
Facsimile: 316.733.7103
e-mail: books@ASRpublishing.com
website: ASRpublishing.com

Designed by Pulaski Design Studio, Wichita, Kansas
Printed in the United States of America by Mennonite Press, Newton, Kansas

ISBN 0-9663673-3-2

Library of Congress Catalog Card Number: 98-070703

Table of Contents

Acknowledgments

I credit three people for my success in fund raising. Fund raising and the management of philanthropy always have come easily to me. However, each of the following persons contributed greatly to my success. Their guidance, support, and instruction — though not necessarily long in duration or deep in understanding — was very significant.

Arthur Frantzreb has served over the years as my counselor, mentor and friend. His guidance during a $100 million campaign in the late 1980s was key to its success. Art gave us fund raisers permission to think "out of the box." He encouraged creativity in gift packaging. Art recognized the end result was the enabling of institutional mission for the long term, not the counting of dollars.

Ken Smith was President of the Kansas Independent College Fund when we had lunch almost 20 years ago. Ken, an optimist, encouraged setting challenges and then surpassing those challenges. Ken has been retired for many years, but periodically shares with me his thoughts on philanthropy.

John Green invited me to be Vice President for Development at Washburn University in the early '80s. He offered me a job that included alumni, public, media and legislative relations. As our conversation was coming to a close, he said, "Oh yeah, and I want you to raise $21 million." That afterthought began my career. I thank John for the courage of his confidence. While his tenure as President was controversial, it should be gratifying to him to know that the President of the Foundation at Washburn has expressed on more than one occasion that the University is benefiting now from gifts that began during our earlier tenure together.

Others who have influenced my philanthropic thinking have included David Dunlop at Cornell, Warren Armstrong at Wichita State University, Darrell Wyrick at the University of Iowa, and Murray Blackwelder at Iowa State University. Thanks are due to Murray, too, for his generous words, which are quoted on the cover of this book. Equally important are the donors and clients who have trusted me and given me confidence. They are many and varied. They have become friends, and I value each and every one.

My editor, Joan Mitchell, has been vital and important in teaching me more about writing because writing did not come to me as naturally as fund raising. Like many, I know, I have opinions and thoughts, but am sometimes unable to put those thoughts into words. Eight years ago, I was encouraged by the mother of my son, Austin, to dictate my thoughts on fund raising and then re-write them over and over until they conveyed what I wanted. Karin was right; it worked.

Shelly Chinberg, who has served as my assistant for years, has been diligent in providing support for my many rewrites. Christine Wheat has provided support in researching and organizing the success stories in the final chapter.

Now with more than 60 articles published in a wide variety of the popular fund-raising media, touching on strategy, cultivation, prospect identification, and closing a gift (the subject of this collection), I have been gratified by the response. One reader told me she put the "Twenty-Nine Secrets of Closing That Gift" on her bulletin board and reviews them daily. Another told me that he looks forward to my writing, because it is creative and practical information. Just in the last week I have learned my work has been translated into Spanish. I am humbled by these comments.

This book and the lessons it seeks to impart, would not have been possible without the help and friendship of those I've named here, as well hundreds of colleagues, clients and friends. Thank you, all.

Bob Hartsook
March 1998

Foreword

The one question I have been asked most often throughout my career is "How do you ask people for those big gifts?" My answer is simple: The donors believe their gifts will make a difference, that they will improve people's lives. It really is just that simple.

Frequently, that response is not sufficiently concrete to help fund raisers eager to continually improve their success rate and professional performance. Therefore, I have prepared this collection of articles to share my thoughts on the whole range of solicitation issues. Evaluating success in fund raising is easy: Either you close the gift or you don't. This book is about closing successfully.

The articles have been organized in an attempt to allow you to get the most out of these concepts. Ultimately, closing is the result of proper preparation. The last section, "Where It Works," puts together the concepts with behind-the-scenes discussions of five very successful campaigns.

You may have heard me say that nobody wants to give money away, yet millions of people want to change people's lives. This is the foundation of my philanthropic philosophy. It has served me well. More important, it has served my clients well.

Additionally, I believe that we as fund raisers have much to learn, and that continuing to learn is one of our highest professional obligations. As a result, I admonish all and remind myself to do the following when considering a solicitation and eventually closing the gift:

1. ***Listen to your donor.*** They will tell you much if you practice the art of careful listening.

2. ***Demonstrate the gift's impact.*** It is important to be clear in demonstrating how their gift will make a difference. Remember a presentation without a demonstration is merely a conversation.

3. ***Think of everyone you meet as a prospect.*** Even before *The Millionaire Next Door*, we knew of millions of people who had wealth and wanted to make a difference; don't look past them.

4. ***Stay close to your mission.*** There is so much money out there that we sometimes try to be all things to all people. Do what you do well.

When we suggest that a reader, after following the strategies in this book, will be successful 99% of the time, it is because we believe proper identification, research, cultivation and preparation will reveal much of a donor's capability and intent to give.

This is not to say that it is easy. It is not. But reliance, purely, on the fund-raising axiom, "People don't give if they aren't asked," can lead to frustration, discouragement, diminished confidence and, yes, a gift or two. Success is more than asking. Success is closing the gift at the highest reasonable level. Good luck! No, that's wrong; follow these strategies and you'll make your own luck.

You will find in this book that we have frequently changed the name of a donor or an institution, because of the donor's or institution's desire for confidentiality.

Ten years ago I was encouraged to put my thoughts in writing. To those who encouraged me, I say thank you. Through over 60 published articles in a wide variety of fund-raising publications, and now with this book, I hope I have contributed to our dialogue.

I hope you enjoy your review of my gift-closing thoughts, and that in some ways they help you become a more effective fund raiser. Call me, if I can help.

Bob Hartsook
March 1998

P.S. The response to this book has been overwhelming. Schools have used it as text, organizations have used it to train volunteers, professionals have called to say what an easy and quick tool it is for fund raising. We are all gratified.

June 1999 second printing

Chapter 1:

A Win/Win Success

The five articles in this section outline the essential elements of philanthropic solicitation. If preparation of the prospect has been appropriate and reasonable — Do they know you? Do you know them? Do they know your cause? Do they know the need for financial support? — you can expect a "yes" 99 percent of the time. You can close that gift.

"Twenty-Nine Secrets to Closing That Gift" reminds the experienced fund raiser of those elements necessary for success. The article helps the novice fund raiser to organize and prepare for solicitations. We hope some "secrets" are very obvious. For example, telling the truth should not have to be a part of the article, but it is. Also included are being prepared, being sincere, being professional, etc.

However prepared a fund raiser may be, mistakes are inevitable. "Top Ten Solicitation Mistakes," takes you through the problems that have been identified as major mistakes in the solicitation process. Issues such as talking too much and not fully understanding your donor's capability are discussed in a candid, straightforward manner.

USA Today reported several years ago that a beggar on the street was successful in solicitations 50 percent of the time. Each fund raiser should expect and receive a higher level of accomplishment. After all, the beggar does not have the benefit of prospect research, solicitation training, etc. In fact, experience dictates that if you follow the 13 strategies suggested in "How to be Successful 99 Percent of the Time," you will be.

Our firm has been well recognized for finding donors and gifts where others do not. The article "How to Get a Million-Dollar Gift and Have the Donor Thank You!" is a step-by-step measure of how to bring in the big gift.

These five articles provide you with the tools to understand how successful solicitations should be organized. You are on your way to closing that gift.

Twenty-Nine Secrets to Closing That Gift

These principles can — and should — become second nature to any fund raiser. Practicing them will make major gift solicitations a win-win deal.

A successful solicitation at any giving level involves many considerations. As fund raisers, we often have heard the story of a large gift donor's response when asked, "Why did you make such a large gift to that institution?" The response, "Well, they asked." You closed that gift!

Of course, as professional fund raisers, we know it's not as simple as that.

We must come to the understanding that no one wants just to give away money; but rather, provide support for children, wildlife, senior citizens, cultural endeavors, educational opportunities and the wide variety of other community interests.

We must hold ourselves responsible for our successes and failures as fund raisers. In order for us to be successful, we must decide that we are going to step forward and, as we have heard many times, ask for the gift.

Here are 29 principles that can — and should — become second nature to any fund raiser. The practice of these principles will increase substantially the successful solicitation of gifts.

1. ***Set reasonable and achievable goals.*** Set both long- and short-term goals for yourself as well as your development operation. Then, develop strategies on how to achieve those goals.

2. ***Maintain a positive attitude toward yourself as well as your prospects.*** A positive outlook on life is a constant daily regimen.

3. ***Believe in yourself and your institution.*** We have all heard the saying "If you don't; who will?" You must believe wholeheartedly in your institution and the service it provides the non-profit arena. If you don't believe in your institution, neither will your prospect. Your conviction — or lack thereof — will be evident to all potential funders.

4. ***Learn and execute the fundamentals of solicitation.*** The solicitation process is a talent that can only come through practice and new information. Read. Attend seminars. Develop mentor relationships.

5. ***Understand your prospect and meet his or her needs.*** Generally, we spend too much time telling what we have to offer, and too little time finding out what our prospects need.

6. ***Establish long-term relationships.*** Remember the golden rule: Treat others as you want to be treated. As you get to know your prospect, you will learn the best ways to serve that person. It is important for you to be honest and candid. It is your responsibility to show your prospect ways in which philanthropy can meet his or her desires and ambitions. Once you accomplish that objective, you will have a loyal donor.

7. *Be prepared.* Self motivation and preparation are the life-blood of your efforts. You must be eager and ready to explain why individuals should give to your institution. Be prepared to answer questions and respond to criticism.

8. *Professional appearance.* Remember that looking professional can reflect very positively on you and your institution.

9. *Strive to establish rapport and confidence.* As you get to know the prospect, work to develop early confidence.

10. *Master the information.* If you do not know your institution inside and out, there is no way you will be free to solicit an appropriate gift. You need background to have confidence in the ask and to make it stick.

11. *Tell the truth.* If you tell the truth, you will never have to remember what was said.

12. *Be sincere.* When you are sincere about helping people, it shows.

13. *Sell the impact, not the means.* So often we spend time telling people the various tricky ways in which they can make a gift rather than reminding them of the impact their gifts can have on people's lives. When that occurs, we are no different than those selling products in a retail store. Fund raising, while it follows many sales techniques, is not retail sales.

14. *Qualify the prospect.* Don't waste time working with someone who does not have sufficient interest in your institution or lacks the financial capacity.

15. *Never put down other agencies or fund raisers.* You might be tempted to share with prospects insights you have gained regarding other agencies or fund raisers. This will reflect badly on you in the long run.

16. **Be on time.** When you are tardy, in effect you are saying, "I don't respect your time." There is no excuse for being late. If you are going to be late, call ahead and apologize.

17. **Use humor.** Humor is one of the best means of raising money. More than anything else, having fun at what I do and making the prospect laugh, have helped me to be successful in this field.

18. **Use testimonials.** There is nothing stronger than having a satisfied donor who is excited about the institution and its impact to serve as a reference to your prospect.

19. **Ask for the gift.** I know we have heard it many times, but so often when we analyze why a solicitation has been unsuccessful it is because we never really asked for the gift.

20. **When you make a promise — keep it.** If you are not able to fulfill a promise to a prospect, that person will not trust you. As a result, you will not be able to move them up the giving ladder.

21. **Get along with others.** Closing a gift is a team effort. Usually, there are others involved in the process leading up to the solicitation, including those involved in prospect identification, research and cultivation. Make them feel a part of your successes and failures.

22. **After you ask for the gift — shut up.** Nothing else needs to be said. If the donor does not make the gift, make plans for a future relationship. When a gift does not succeed, try to learn something from the solicitation. How could I have done it better? What

other information could have been brought to the table? What did I learn about the prospect?

23. *Conduct each solicitation passionately*. The more thorough you are in the identification and cultivation processes, the better chance you have to be successful in the solicitation.

24. *Don't blame others when the fault is yours.* Accept responsibility. Then do something about it.

25. *Follow up.* Make certain you keep in contact with your prospect. Do whatever it takes. It will take many exposures before you finally will get a gift.

26. *Learn how to accept rejection.* Remember that rejection of a gift is not a rejection of you. It is merely a rejection of your gift opportunity.

27. *Be creative.* Once you have learned the fundamentals of your institution and your work, think of ways to set yourself apart from the competition.

28. *Learn the power of persistence.* When someone rejects your offer, recognize that your persistence eventually will pay off.

29. *Don't brag about your gifts.* While you spend time telling everyone about the latest big gift you secured for your institution, someone else is out there soliciting a bigger one for another institution.

I hope these pointers give you insight and food for thought as you review how you go about closing that gift. Many gifts are lost because these simple principles are not followed.

Examine them and make everyone an integral part of your solicitation process. Concentrate on making your weaknesses your strengths. The rewards will be forthcoming — not only in terms of your own self-esteem, but more important, in terms of the successes you will have in fulfilling your donors' objectives. Congratulations on closing that gift!

Top Ten Solicitation Mistakes

All fund raisers know that unless you ask, you will not get a gift. But between the decision to ask for the gift and the actual solicitation, many problems can arise.

Allison Zook became responsible for the fund raising at the Known Children's Services Program (KCSP). KCSP had a need of nearly $1 million annually. Year after year, her success came up short of the goal. At the conclusion of three years on the job, Allison was released from her responsibilities. When she looked back on what she had been doing with donors, this test might have been helpful.

Here are 10 common mistakes that can be devastating to the successful completion of a gift. Ask yourself these questions.

1. ***Do you talk too much — never listen?*** Frequently, because of the enthusiasm to communicate the importance of the project, program or institution, fund raisers talk too much to the prospective donor without ever listening to what the donor wants or expects for the project.

2. ***Do you answer unasked questions?*** In asking for a gift, do you immediately say something like, "We

know we are asking a lot, and you may not be able to meet it, but anything you can give would be appreciated."? A comment such as this immediately lowers the size of the gift.

3. ***Do you assume the donor has consented to a gift without ever actually asking for a specific gift?*** At times, a fund raiser can over-read a donor's statements, body signals, etc.

4. ***Do you fail to follow up?*** When donors express the need to discuss the gift with a spouse, business associates, etc., do you wait for the donor to contact you when a decision has been made? We have heard donors say repeatedly that their gift must not have been too important since no one came back to ask for it.

5. ***Do you not know whether the donor can make this gift, but you ask anyway?*** Within reasonable limitations, you can know whether the donor has the economic capacity to make a gift. Economic impact alone does not assure a gift, but it makes you confident with the ask.

6. ***Do you fail to push for an end?*** As your presentation closes, are you able to move the donor to the point of indicating that they will make a decision, and when?

7. ***Do you fail to build up to the ask?*** Do you immediately ask for the gift without building rapport and understanding, and reminding potential donors about the opportunities of the campaign or project?

8. ***Are you acting like a beggar?*** Never be ashamed to ask others to support a worthy project. Have you forgotten that this project is important and will change people's lives? Very few people will be responsive to a fund raiser who seems like a beggar.

9. ***Do you know what it takes to make this gift happen?*** Have you listened to the donor and tailored your proposal in accordance? Have you utilized the appropriate phrases and outlined the means by which that donor wants to make this gift?

10. ***Do you approach prospective donors without a gift strategy?*** Do you treat all donors the same, without recognizing that each has his or her own particular view of life?

These 10 mistakes are commonly made by fund raisers. If any of these are familiar, you may want to make immediate adjustments. Such changes can result in a more successful solicitation record.

How to be Successful 99 Percent of the Time

A study, reported in *USA Today* suggested that a beggar on the street received a gift 50 percent of the time. Surely, we as fund raisers are at least as good as beggars — they may develop instincts for people, but they do not have the opportunity to learn intellectual skills such as prospect research, prospect profile, solicitation training, etc.

What we want ideally, is the right person asking the right person for the right project for the right amount. Most of the time when we fail in a solicitation, it is because the wrong person is asking the wrong person for the wrong project for the wrong amount. If any part of the equation is "wrong," we set ourselves up to fail.

In fund raising we always are looking for opportunities to be successful. We know that a gift occurs as a result of an individual having the economic capacity to make a gift and the desire and intent strong enough to make the gift occur.

There are a number of important guiding principles that, if followed specifically, can guide you to success most of the time. These principles include the following:

1. *Care about your institution and programs.* Have a dream. Think about the leadership's vision. Understand and appreciate that donors are interested in making a difference in people's lives. Make sure you have created the opportunity for them to have that kind of impact.

2. *Recognize that it is the donor's money and not yours.* They do not have to give it away, with the exception of foundations, and even in the case of foundations they can make choices. We must honor the donor's right to choose and demonstrate that we appreciate and value their level of confidence in us.

3. *Look at everyone you meet as a prospect.* All too often, the wealth of this country is hidden, because many of those who control extraordinary levels of wealth do not carry it on their sleeve or make it available. Therefore, it is important always to be looking and thinking about those who could serve as prospects.

4. *Listen to your donor and think about their priorities.* What do they care about? What do they believe will be the impact of their gift? Listen to the way they want to change people's lives.

5. *Focus on why this project makes a difference.* Focus on why this project is important. Focus on how this project changes people's lives. Focus, focus, focus.

6. *Discover ways to demonstrate the impact this project can have and the role the donor can play.* A good friend once told me that a presentation without a demonstration is merely a conversation. If you want to be able to close this gift, you need to demonstrate to the donor the level of impact his or her gift can have.

7. *Acknowledge, appreciate, recognize and value even the opportunity to share with potential donors information regarding this project.* It is important that they understand that their time, interest, understanding and values are as important as their money.

8. *Be creative in how the donor's resources can be brought to the table.* We all know that if we ask for $100,000, we would like a check for $100,000. However, it is important to remember that there are a variety of ways we can assist donors in making the donation of that gift as easy as possible.

9. *Have a sense of humor.* Enjoy yourself, your donor and the project. Fund raising has a tendency to become very serious. And while our projects are serious, it also is important that we enjoy what we are doing. To enjoy it, you must have a sense of humor.

10. *Stay very close to your mission.* Do not chase dollars. Do not just go after people who have money. Remember your mission is what drives your institution. The closer you remain to the mission, the more successful you will be.

11. *Study your prospect for the proper time to make the solicitation.* Even the donor who is most inclined to make a gift has particular times that they are more open to solicitation. Think about that timing and be careful in your solicitation.

12. *Solicit the gift orally and in writing at the same time.* It is important for a donor to hear you say, "We would like a gift of $10,000." In addition, it is important that the terms of the gift — pledge period, recognition, etc. — be in writing for the donor to consider when you are gone.

13. When a donor says, "I am interested in the project and will give the gift consideration,"— follow up.
We have heard from so many donors that little or no follow up results in no gift.

These 13 ideas are tried and true ways in which our consultants and clients have been successful in bringing philanthropic life to the institutions and projects with which they have been involved.

You should be able to improve your success rate substantially — perhaps to 99 percent — by using these strategies. If we can do it, you can, too.

Step Up to Major Gifts

Here are five steps to follow to make sure the solicitation process succeeds.

Making the best solicitation is critical to the successful fund-raising program. Fund raisers who have achieved the highest levels of giving by donors solicit those persons who have the wealth, care about the philanthropy and can make the decision.

Here are the five steps to that solicitation process.

1. *Match the solicitor and the donor.* Have the best person make the call for the solicitation. Don't take one person's word that he or she is the best to solicit. Test the idea of who is the best match with several sources.

2. *Call on the decision maker.* Call on the person who will make the decision. Make your initial call with the top person. If your research says you meet with husband and wife — then meet with them. If you are told the president of the company makes the decision — meet with the president. Meeting with non-decision makers could delay or impede a successful solicitation.

3. *Prepare for objections.* Be prepared for the list of objections to the proposal. There are really no

objections that are valid except the prospect does not care about your project. Be prepared to show how your project meets his or her philanthropic priorities.

4. *Ask for the gift.* Recognize the time when it becomes apparent. When the prospect starts asking how this project will impact the community or a particular constituency, it may be time to go for the solicitation. Look for natural ways to link the project and the prospect. Ask for the order! Ask for the gift!

5. *Close the gift.* Don't leave until you have closed the proposal. The following approaches have been used for closing a gift request.

> *"I am confident ..."*
> *"I'd like to have your decision so we may continue to help..."*
> *"I'm going to ask for your commitment ..."*
> *"How soon can we announce your gift?"*
> *"Can we discuss how we want to recognize you for this gift?"*

If you are unable to close the gift, always keep control by indicating you will be in touch in the next two or three days.

Congratulations on receiving the top gift!

How to Get a Million-Dollar Gift and Have the Donor Thank You!

"Since you asked, I guess we'll do it." This is how a love affair began between Harry and Lucy and the Harry and Lucy Student Center at a local youth program. In fact, it was Lucy who said, "Gee, I'm so happy you asked us."

Another donor, who made a multi-million endowment gift, announced to a group of faculty and students recently, "I was selected to make this gift and, therefore, it became my School of Communications. There would have been a communications school regardless of my gift, but it wouldn't have been from me. I am thankful for the opportunity to have made such a gift."

These people represent just a few of the many who are pleased to be asked. You may think it's rare, but it isn't.

The following are illustrations of ways in which you can position your project and campaign so that your donors may thank you for their gifts.

1. *Have a Vision.* Make sure you are supporting a worthwhile project with a future vision that will have an impact on people's lives.

2. *Go to Your Prospects.* Think seriously about prospective donors who possess both the capacity to make gifts at a significant level and the caring or interest to make the project succeed.

3. *Stimulate Interest.* Develop cultivation strategies that have the potential to increase the donor's level of appreciation for the project. (Generally, there is not much we, as fund raisers, can do about a donor's economic capacity to make a gift, but we can seriously impact his or her level of interest and enthusiasm.)

4. *Make the Project Their Project.* Engage the prospects in developing the case for support. People support what they help create; therefore, the opportunity to encourage them to become a part of your organization is key to success.

5. *Give the Donor a Familiar Face.* Encourage members of the project's staff to get to know the donor and share their dreams for the program. Those who work day-to-day to continue the program for the clients have a great message to send to donors about the importance of the project.

6. *Remember People.* People give to people. Make sure the right person is identified to solicit the gift.

7. *Appreciation is Always Necessary.* Extend appreciation, acknowledgment, and value to the donors for their support and interest. It always is important that the donors know you respect the amount of time they have spent learning about the project and appreciating its value.

8. *Be Clear About What You Want.* Solicit the gift orally and in writing. It is important for the donors to hear you make a gift request at a certain dollar level. It also is important to delineate clearly the proposal in writing in terms of how the gift is to be made and the recognition to be expected.

9. *Be Creative.* Support the donors in their quest to accomplish this gift. Show them that you can create various opportunities to secure the gift.

Having a donor thank you for making a gift may sound strange. However, virtually every donor of a major gift ought to feel great satisfaction in his or her gift, and realize that someone had to bring them to this opportunity. As a result of their giving, lives will be changed significantly and opportunities created.

Chapter 2:

Closing Estate Gifts

Closing a gift through an estate is a unique means of establishing a contribution. Statistics say that as much as $50 - 100 billion is being generated annually in gift designations through estates. Simple wills continue to be the most significant means by which estate gifts occur. The key is to not be put off by the more complex planned-gift instruments.

The three articles in this section provide numerous illustrations of how these gifts are packaged and developed. Creativity is one of the most important components of a successful deferred- and estate-gift solicitation.

"Pulling In the Assets" describes real-life circumstances that five families used to transfer their assets to nonprofit organizations. Looking for low-income-producing assets and idle assets is one painless means to secure large gifts. Lessons are clear that donors who do not have children are prospects for terrific gifts.

When you look at "Nurturing Deferred Gifts," you learn that families without children are growing at a rapid rate. The technical component of this method is not as key as the relationships that are encouraged.

Very importantly, "The Donor as a Customer" reminds us of the two rules when dealing with a donor. Rule #1: The donor is always right. Rule #2: When in doubt, review Rule #1.

Planned giving is an arrow that any good fund raiser should have in his or her quiver.

Pulling In the Assets

The thought of dealing with planned giving stirs anxiety in the minds of many fund raisers. Perhaps they do not really grasp the technicalities of the process or they may think the donors will be "turned off" by it. Yet planned giving should be one of the significant arrows in the quiver of any good development officer.

By definition, planned giving is a method by which individuals make a commitment of their assets that generally materialize following their death. Or it may involve use of assets organized and constructed in an unusual manner to create lifetime benefits to the donor with ultimate benefit to the institution.

No major gift should be solicited without the inclusion of an estate vehicle or the suggestion of how the inclusion of an estate vehicle could assist the donor as well as the institution in their long-term plans. The use of this strategy has resulted in numerous significant gifts.

Here are some real-life examples (though the names have been changed) of how this was accomplished:

Jack Norton

Jack Norton was a young entrepreneur who had garnered substantial funds in his lifetime through the marketing of a new idea that became widely accepted.

Mr. Norton decided it would be valuable to use his wealth to construct a new facility at the state university he attended. In the development of the capital gift — which amounted to $1.5 million — the university suggested that the quality and long-term vitality of the new facility could be enhanced substantially if Norton and his wife would consider the inclusion of an endowment to maintain the facility following their deaths. The donor and his wife, enthusiastic about how the building began emerging as a significant statement for the university, added a $6 million endowment as a deferred component to benefit maintenance, anticipated renovation and the long-term viability of the facility.

Lesson: *The donor was asked to make an estate provision at the time that he and his wife were at the highest point of excitement and energy over their new capital investment.*

The Apples

John and Yvonne Apple were advanced in years and had accumulated a significant sum of money over their lifetime. Historically good donors, they decided to assist their church in building a new education wing for the church's young people. In the development of their gift, the Apples were advised not to look at just the level of income they could pledge to this campaign, but at whatever assets might generate resources that could be effectively used.

In reviewing their assets, the Apples mentioned a farm that had produced well for them over the years, but that they believed could produce at a much higher level or could be converted to cash. The Apples decided to give the farm to the church as a part of a lead trust, allowing the church to sell. The church would use the income only from the next 10 years' proceeds to fund the new building.

The asset, when sold, amounted to $1.3 million. The income anticipated is approximately $100,000 annually for the next 10 years. In fact, the Apples were able to make a gift of $1 million and then transfer that previous asset to their grandchildren.

Lesson: *Donors should review their entire asset pool in seeking the opportunity to make a substantial gift. Many times non- or low-income producing assets can be transferred to their charity and provide a substantial benefit to both the donor and the institution.*

The Hawks

Mrs. Hawk had been adopted through a local children's home. And, while the children's home had progressed to cover other child-care issues, Mrs. Hawk continued to harbor strong feelings for the institution. Over the years, the Hawks had made many gifts to the children's home in support of various activities and programs.

When the institution was having difficulty meeting its cash flow needs for a new facility, the Hawks offered to loan the children's home $500,000 for two years at no interest. The Hawks' gift, which at competitive rates amounted to nearly $100,000, enabled the children's home to complete its facility without going over budget. It allowed Mrs. Hawk to provide resources to an institution that had helped her when she was in need. The principal was returned to the Hawks, so it did not deplete their assets.

Lesson: *Idle assets or assets producing excess earnings can be utilized on a temporary basis by charities. In this way, donors provide interim assistance, but do not permanently deplete their asset base. Frequently, donors eventually give the loaned asset because they get used to living without it.*

The Whites

In another scenario, a lead gift was needed for a new performance hall. The agency turned to the Whites. The Whites enjoyed a high profile in the community and, as a result, had been solicited by virtually every agency in the area. But few people realized the involvement and deep feelings the Whites had for the theater.

The agency asked for a $500,000 lead gift on behalf of the performing arts center. The Whites in turn responded that they could not make that gift as a cash gift, but were willing to review their assets to determine if there were other ways to meet the request. As a result of their review, the Whites made a gift of $200,000 cash, non-income-producing farmland worth $150,000, and another $150,000 as a contract to the will.

The performing arts center was a new organization. Securing a $500,000 lead gift was critical to its success. Had the agency been unable to accept the land and the contract against the will, it would have received only $200,000 cash and run the risk of not meeting the campaign's goals.

Lesson: *Using non-income producing assets, future gifts and cash gifts can help donors reach the size of gifts needed to produce pace-setting goals.*

The Arnolds

People are likely to make planned-giving decisions during life-changing events such as birth, death, marriage, divorce and even travel. Such was the case with Mildred and Clifford Arnold.

The Arnolds were about to embark on an extended trip to Australia. In light of this trip, they decided it would be appropriate for them to revisit their estate plan and, in particular, their will. As a result of that review, Mrs. Arnold made the decision to create a bequest to fund a small scholarship that she had initiated at a university in their community. This arrangement, however, included more than the simple identification of a bequest.

First, the ultimate-beneficiary proceeds of a spend-thrift trust was changed to benefit the university. Eventually, a $500,000 bequest was made to the institution. A dean of the university as well as the president recognized the importance of this gift and began to include the Arnolds in all of the university's activities. Mrs. Arnold now has made cash gifts in advance of her death of more than $150,000, satisfying a portion of her bequest.

Lesson: *When estate gifts are made, good stewardship of the gift and involvement of the donor might well result in advancement of the proceeds of the estate.*

Mr. Jackson

Mr. Jackson had just lost his wife. She had been ill for a long time. The very day of her passing, he was approached about providing an important lead gift for his church's capital campaign. The capital gift request was $500,000.

Mr. Jackson was in the mood to discuss his philanthropy that day as well as the importance of the church in his and his wife's life. During that discussion, he made a decision to create an endowment of $1 million through his estate for the benefit of the church. Furthermore, because the minister reminded him of the importance of his annual contributions, Mr. Jackson pledged to sustain his annual commitment at $110,000 for the next five years; a total of $550,000.

So, through an initial request of $500,000, the minister was successful in receiving a long-term estate commitment of $1 million and a sustaining annual commitment of $550,000. In one day, through one call, through three different means, the church was enriched economically with $2,050,000.

Lesson: *When discussing capital or endowment giving, remind the donors of the need for their continuing annual relationship. Secure a long-term pledge of that gift at the same time.*

What common threads run through all of these donors?

1. Many did not have children and those who did already had provided for them in other ways.

2. Most were thinking about the present and future needs of the institution or church they supported.

3. Their intensity of involvement was very high or had the ability to become very high.

4. Finally, they were willing to learn about the intricacies of planned gifts in order to help their institutions.

The fear that fund raisers feel towards planned gifts stems from the focus on the technology and technicalities of the process. Put the focus on planned giving back where it belongs. People give because they have the resources to make a gift and the institution is appropriate for them. It's up to creative professionals to help prospective donors find vehicles to satisfy their desired giving level.

Nurturing Deferred Gifts

Deferred giving is viewed as the fastest-growing field of philanthropy in America. As our population grows older, the country's wealth increases substantially. The number of single and childless families increases each year; according to census studies, the number of non-family households will grow by 50 percent, to 23 percent of the total population. It is no coincidence that the creation of gifts through estate-planning mechanisms is gaining favor.

For simplicity, a deferred gift may be defined as one in which the assets designated by the donor come to the benefit of the nonprofit at the death of the donor. There are, of course, deferred and planned gifts in which the assets come to the nonprofit earlier. Strategies for the nurturing aspect of the planned gift apply to these gifts as well.

Significant attention usually is given to the structuring and technical preparation of deferred and planned gifts. Many fund raisers are asked to learn highly sophisticated technical means by which deferred gifts may be established. While a background in this area is important, it is of more importance that the nonprofit staff person not become so intertwined with the structuring of deferred gifts that it causes future questions concerning conflicts of interest. So rather than becoming overwhelmed with technical aspects of deferred giving, the fund raiser would better use time encouraging, nurturing, cultivating, marketing and closing deferred gifts. Following are seven crucial steps necessary for the acquisition of deferred gifts. Note that they do not involve significant technical knowledge.

1. ***Define the kind of deferred gifts the organization is willing to receive.*** Not all agencies will accept every kind of deferred gift. Define the types of deferred and planned gifts your agency will accept.

   Most fund raisers are aware of the wide variety of print materials designed as planned and deferred-gift marketing tools. Many of them are very well done and highly sophisticated. Planned-gift officers frequently are told that they simply need to buy one of the these packages, distribute them and the planned gifts will roll in.

   Certainly, there is an important role for printed planned-gift marketing devices. If you subscribe to a campaign, make sure your agency is prepared to administer the types of planned gifts that might result from that marketing. Remember the story of Jack Smith.

   Jack had been a regular contributor to a national social-service agency. It was not unusual for Jack to create a $10,000 gift annuity on an annual basis to that organization. One summer, Jack received promotional materials for his local hospital foundation. The hospital promoted a wide variety of deferred gifts. Because of Jack's previous deferred giving to the national social-service organization, he contacted the hospital and indicated that he was interested in making a $10,000 gift annuity. After the development officer stuttered and put him on hold, she finally got back on the line to report that the hospital did not administer gift annuities.

Imagine the level of credibility that hospital foundation now had with Jack for any other kind of gift. Obviously, the lesson is to market only those aspects of deferred giving that you are prepared to administer.

2. ***Bring together experts in the field as advisors.*** The field of deferred and planned giving is an ever-changing, highly technical field. There are good reasons why you, as the fund raiser, should not get deeply immersed in the technical aspects. In order to provide the level of support and sophistication necessary, create a deferred-gift advisory panel or committee. This group should consist of a community-recognized lawyer, CPA, senior insurance professional, financial planner and bank trust officer. In certain fund-raising markets, real estate professionals and stock brokers also might be good additions.

The purpose of the deferred-gift advisory panel is three-fold.

  a. To educate one another on the various techniques of each profession in terms of deferred-gift approaches.

  b. To provide a resource for counsel and support as deferred-gift opportunities arise.

  c. To inform community leaders who will come in contact with deferred-giving prospects of the availability and desire of your nonprofit to receive such gifts.

3. *Watch for life-changing events to drive the deferred gift.* Deferred-gift planning by the donor does not occur at particular times during the year, but at life-changing times. People review their estate plans at marriage, birth, death, divorce, sickness, and before periods of significant travel. Therefore, you need to place your nonprofit in front of these prospects on a regular basis.

The prospect pool primarily is composed of those donors who are in the estate-planning period of their lives. These prospects are generally more than 45 to 50 years of age, but generally not beyond 70 to 75. The task is to identify prospects — friends of your institution — who fit those age-qualified categories. To narrow the prospect pool even more, look for those prospects who fit the age category and do not have children.

The perceived wealth and affluence of a prospective donor is not a determining criterion for deferred gifts. Deferred gifts are gifts that can be created from existing assets, as asset replenishment, etc. It is not unusual for those persons without natural heirs, even though their estates may appear small, to have an estate of $250,000 to $500,000.

4. *Get your simple message to your prospects regularly.* We encourage the development of a simple and tasteful marketing message to be distributed three times a year to this prospect pool. This newsletter should contain an article or two about a particular type of fund raising through gifts such as wills, life insurance, etc.; a testimonial from someone who has made a deferred gift to your organization about his excitement and satisfaction; and a response card.

All response cards should ask for at least two things: more information about a particular method of deferred giving; and an opportunity for the donor to indicate that they already have included the agency in their will, trust, life insurance, etc.

5. *Recognize that the deferred-gift prospect is unique and special.* The follow-up on a prospect for a deferred gift is a delicate process. The *Planned Gifts Counselor* newsletter suggests five ways to deal with these prospects, since many are of a mature age level.

   a. Practice patience. You will need to give these prospects extra time in making their decision.

   b. Make sure you are heard. These are complex and sensitive issues. Make sure you have explained the opportunity in a simple way and explained the impact their gift might have on the agency. Do not be patronizing. Sometimes our efforts to be courteous or understanding might be misinterpreted as patronizing. Be careful!

   c. Allow time for reflection. Recognize that their decision-making abilities will be slower than normal. Give them time to think through the issues. Suggest the use of support from a spouse, trusted friend or counselor.

   d. Be totally honest. Persons who have reached this point of making their estate-planning decisions are interested in credibility and integrity. Do not move too rapidly or you will be classified with the "losers" they have encountered in their lives and quickly be dismissed.

   e. Ask for the gift. Like other forms of solicitation, have a specific project in mind that their gift eventually can support. You must prepare the case well and be able to demonstrate clearly the impact that gift will have in the future.

Share with them a reasonable dollar amount that will have the level of impact they are expecting. Remember, sometimes their perspective on dollar values today may change by the time that gift comes to your agency 10 to 20 years from now.

6. ***Don't forget to recognize and acknowledge the gift.*** Nothing will irritate a donor more than to have the deferred gift relegated to something less significant than an outright gift. When people go through the trouble and effort of creating an estate plan that includes your agency, they see that as "dollars" they are giving to your nonprofit and expect appropriate recognition.

Successful deferred-gift programs recognize deferred gifts and give them an appropriate place for acknowledgement in the overall scheme of fund raising. We encourage special giving clubs for deferred gifts as well as actuarialized charts for discounting the value of the gift to present-day values.

7. ***Remember to maintain contact with the donor.*** Even though the deferred gift will not materialize for many years, many fund raisers have found that annual giving has increased from those persons who have made deferred gifts. These persons have enjoyed learning about the agency and watching it grow over their lifetime. Therefore, they may provide additional funds in advance of their estate gifts.

In some cases, deferred-gift donors have prepaid their deferred gifts. This occurred in a deferred gift by one donor to Colby Community College in Kansas for a Fine Arts Center for which she advance-paid her estate gift of $250,000. This also was the case with a donor to Washburn University in Topeka, Kansas. She advanced $100,000 on an endowment scholarship campaign gift that she had made many years before. While this is not the standard and will not happen in every case, it happens enough times that it is worthy of acknowledgement and cultivation.

If successful, you have done something very important in your deferred-gift donor's life. In many cases these individuals have not identified actual objects of their gifts. By your shaping this vision, they can share the excitement that their gift will have an important impact on the future of your institution.

The Donor as a Customer
Put the Donor's Objectives First

Frequently, when explaining planned-gift opportunities, we focus on the techniques or pattern of the gift rather than the motivation or need of the donor. This issue was of great concern to the leadership of the capital campaign of the First Presbyterian Church of Waco, Texas. Their campaign — which was to erase a $1.2 million debt on a new education wing, renovate an existing building and add $800,000 in future gifts primarily for endowment — targeted prospects for gifts through estate-planning instruments.

In an effort to simplify planned-giving options for their prospective donors, a simple grid (The Perry Grid) was developed focusing on the donor's need. Once the donor's need has been assessed, The Perry Grid provides a corresponding deferred-gift vehicle that will best meet the donor's objective. Also included is a second option that will allow the donor's objective to occur.

The chart at the top of the next page shows the basic Perry Grid used in their deferred-giving program.

The following is a simple explanation of the five deferred-gift vehicles utilized in the chart.

Donor's Objective	How to Achieve Objective	
	Best Way	**Second Best Way**
1. Increase current income	Charitable Gift Annuity	Charitable Remainder Unitrust
2. Hedge against inflation	Charitable Remainder Trust	Charitable Gift Annuity
3. Income security	Charitable Gift Annuity	Charitable Annuity Trust
4. Current Charitable Deduction	Charitable Annuity Trust	Chaitable Remainder Unitrust
5. Avoid Capital Gains Tax	Charitable Remainder Unitrust	Charitable Annuity Trust
6. Provision for Charity	Charitable Annuity Trust	Charitable Remainder Unitrust
7. Provision for Heirs	Charitable Lead Trust	Wealth Replacement Life Insurance

Charitable Gift Annuity. A donor transfers some amount of cash, securities, or other assets to a nonprofit for the benefit of the nonprofit. In return, the donor receives from the nonprofit a fixed, annual dollar amount as long as he or she lives. The principal remaining after death is the donor's gift to the nonprofit.

Charitable Remainder Unitrust. A donor creates a trust which is managed by a trustee appointed by the donor; such as the nonprofit. The income generated by the trust is paid to one or more beneficiaries specified by the donor, such as the donor, a spouse or children. The beneficiaries receive the income for as long as they live or for a specified number of years, not to exceed twenty. After the lifetime of the beneficiaries, the assets of the trust pass to the nonprofit.

Charitable Annuity Trust. This trust is structured very much like the Unitrust with the major difference being that the beneficiary receives a fixed annual income. It is especially useful when a donor wants to receive a substantial income tax deduction at the time of establishing the Annuity Trust and wants to receive a fixed income for life. The assets pass to the nonprofit.

Charitable Lead Trust. A donor in a high gift- and estate-tax bracket establishes a trust. A fixed annual amount or percentage goes to the nonprofit for the duration of the trust; then the assets of the trust pass to the trust's beneficiaries, such as the donor's heirs. This trust can greatly reduce estate taxes.

Wealth Replacement Life Insurance. A donor would purchase a life insurance policy naming his or her heir as the beneficiary, assuring that the heir receives the gift after the death of the donor. Therefore, the nonprofit is able to receive the gift or the other asset identified for the institution during the donor's lifetime or after the death of the donor.

How to identify a prospect for whom The Perry Grid can be of greatest assistance? The Perry Grid is most useful to individuals who are in early stages of introduction to planned and deferred gifts. They may have simple objectives and may have become frustrated with the various technical ways in which such giving can occur.

Dick Peyton is one individual for whom the Grid worked well. Dick was a government engineer who had accumulated several hundred thousand dollars as a result of good lifetime stewardship and family inheritance. Dick's objective was to make a provision for a charity, but also to provide a hedge against inflation and, as a result, increase his current income. The Perry Grid, utilizing Dick's three motivations or objectives, indicates the use of either a charitable gift annuity or a charitable remainder trust. Since Dick had more than $600,000 that he wanted to set aside, the charitable remainder unitrust became the most appropriate means by which to meet his objectives. Dick made the gift, listing two beneficiaries. He has since passed away. Now those dollars are used to finance the initial construction of a major medical retirement facility.

As another example, Naomi North was interested in providing funds for her heirs. Current income was not of interest. Utilizing The Perry Grid, the charitable lead trust became an obvious means by which the charity could receive an income for a specific period of years. The corpus of the trust would then transfer to her children. Ms. North explored the opportunities of a wealth-replacement life insurance policy which she may still utilize as a means of transferring wealth to her family.

Finally, The Perry Grid has been effective in introducing to the boards of nonprofit institutions the means by which charitable giving through estate planning can assist their institution. The seven simple objectives with several simple alternatives is an easy way to assist board members unschooled in the field of estate planning in their decision-making process.

It is our experience that The Perry Grid can be an effective means to raise substantial dollars, especially when utilized by donors seeking simple answers to simple objectives.

You should always encourage your donor to consult his or her attorney for professional advice.

The Perry Grid of deferred-gift vehicles is the educational tool used by the First Presbyterian Church of Waco, Texas, with each planned-giving prospect.

The success of the First Presbyterian Church campaign also serves as a reminder about our donors as customers: Only by meeting their needs can we be successful in the worthy fund-raising efforts we undertake.

Chapter 3:

Creativity and Cultivation

The two most under-utilized concepts applied in today's philanthropic marketplace are creativity and cultivation. Historically, fund raisers have been only able to see as far as a check or three-year pledge. Working with donors to maximize their assets into a meaningful commitment is an opportunity to make a real contribution.

As fund raisers, we have been told many times that "You don't get the gift if you don't ask." As a result, one may identify the donor and leap immediately to a major gift solicitation.

Between the identification of a donor and solicitation, however, cultivation must occur. Cultivation may mean more to me because I come from an agricultural area. I have watched as good soil has been enriched and prepared. I understand that a wheat crop requires a certain type of fertilizer. I have watched the wheat being put in the soil and cared for with much attention. Finally, I have watched the crop mature into a bountiful harvest. Just as a well-cultivated donor will make a significant gift.

Cultivation is the dimension that is often missing in solicitations today. With proper cultivation a good gift can become an *ultimate* gift.

The three articles to follow are designed to stimulate thinking about the two vital issues of creativity and cultivation in closing a gift.

"Gifts That Go Out of the Box," helps the fund raiser understand that there are a lot of ways to craft a gift. "Practice Your ABCs" is an elementary listing of ways to cultivate a donor. "30 Commandments for Successful Fund Raising" is a reminder of the means to bring intimacy to the donor relationship.

Gifts That Go Out of the Box

We pick up the local paper and learn that Willard Nevin has given $100,000 to a local children's home. "Why, we have been working on Mr. Nevin for years and he always tells us he doesn't have that much money to give away." What made the difference? Could it be how the children's home "planned" the gift?

To add insult to our injury — when asked about the gift, Mr. Nevin replied, "If you had shown me how to make the gift like the children's home did, I would have made it to you." This is your worst nightmare.

When you are considering gift levels of $100,000 or more, high levels of tension and anxiety occur with both the solicitor and the donor. Too often, we do not consider every alternative of how the gift can be made.

Creative strategic planning, commonly called "out-of-the-box thinking," should be applied in fund-raising strategies. Following are ideas on how to accomplish a gift of $100,000 that serves in the best interest of the donor, provides cash flow and opportunity for the recipient, and creates an opportunity that would not have occurred but for a creative idea.

Pledge Payment Over a Term of Years

We would be remiss to open the discussion on creative ways of making gifts without reminding ourselves that we can create opportunities through pledges. This may sound routine, but all too often when we ask a donor for a gift, we forget to tell them that they can pay the pledge out over two, three, four and even five years. Naturally, we create a gift that is easier to complete with annual payments of $20,000 for five years or $33,333 for three years or even $50,000 for two years. The downside is that we do not satisfy all the money needed up front. However, without this pledge opportunity, we might not get the gift at all.

Pledge Payable During a Period of Years

Even the annual pledge payment strategy has its drawbacks in that the donor must be prepared to make annual contributions in equal shares over the two-, three- or five-year period. Many small-business people and entrepreneurs do not know what each year will bring. They often are reluctant to make a commitment because they do not want to be placed in a position of having to tell the executive director, "I can't make my pledge payment this year because business wasn't as good as I had hoped."

We have recommended pledges that allow the payment to be made in whatever increment the donor determines over the agreed-upon pledge period. The only firm pledge is that at the end of the time period, they will have paid (in our example) $100,000. Our experience is that donors want the obligation satisfied. They tend to pay it off early because they do not feel comfortable with what future years might bring.

Quasi Endowment

The term "quasi endowment" creates uneasiness among some fund raisers. However, it is a way to create the impact of $100,000 — and the cash flow of a $100,000 endowment — without taking from the donor the full asset of $100,000. Say we need a $100,000 gift as an endowment that will produce an earning of five percent of the corpus as a distribution to us on an annual basis to fund a program or project. Our prospect could make such a gift, but would rather continue to have access to the $100,000 for her business. She believes that $100,000 could continue to capitalize her entrepreneurial enterprise and could bring great rewards. In her mind, she believes that as a result she could give even more to our institution. No problem!

We suggest a quasi endowment. Under this strategy, we secure an in-perpetuity commitment from the donor for an amount equal to the equivalent value of $100,000 until the donor's death. The donor places in her estate plan that our agency is to receive the equivalent value of $100,000 today in current dollars at her death.

The agency has access to fund the program with the $5,000 (or future equivalent value) in perpetuity as a quasi endowment. Your agency has the value of the endowment for use in your program and the donor can keep her money until she no longer has use for it. If you are unsure of the ability of the donor's estate to fund the value at her death, you may suggest that the donor secure a single-premium life insurance policy to assure the value will be in place.

The basic elements of an endowment are in place. The segregation of the fund and the cash flow are made in order to support the program.

Term Endowment

Term endowment is similar to a quasi endowment, except the donor and the agency agree on a term of years that the equivalency payments will be made. At that time, the donor makes a cash gift of $100,000.

As an example, our Mr. Nevin might want to secure endow a $100,000 project and pay to them one-third of the endowment each year for three years. But in order to activate the endowment, he contributed to the organization the equivalent income value each of the three years and making a difference between their return on the amount of the endowment they had received.

Gift Annuity

A gift annuity, with the donor returning the income, can be a useful tool for a donor who wants the security of knowing she has the income; but really doesn't need it. In this case, the donor gives $100,000 to charity and is provided an income of 9.2 percent or $9,200 per year for her lifetime. The donor gets a significant deduction for the annuity — a portion of the $9,200 is tax free and she gets another deduction for donating the proceeds back.

Stock Gift

We all have heard of donors funding their commitment with stock. It is a good strategy — especially in these times of significant stock appreciation. However, one donor taught me a great lesson. He pledged not cash, but 5,000 shares of a regional bank stock. At the time of the pledge it was the equivalent of $100,000. However, he made it clear that he was not pledging $100,000, rather he was pledging the shares which he would distribute four times over a two-year period.

During the time of the pledge, the bank was purchased and the shares increased in value to more than $131,000. He fulfilled his commitment by making a gift of the shares. This allowed the donor to give a commodity that he knew he could give without concern as to whether the value was $100,000 or not. Obviously, we could have lost in this exchange also, but we might not have received the pledge if it had to be valued at $100,000 regardless.

Summary

All of these are examples of how we respect the donor. After all, it is the donor's money. We allow the donor to set the pattern, pace, method and strategy. Why not? They want us to succeed. We should give them a chance. The alternative is a conservative gift at a level that they are confident can be met.

So our first and second donor who wanted to help, but can't give $100,000, give only $20,000. The third donor who wants to help build an endowment gives us $5,000; even a five-year pledge of $5,000, is only $25,000. The fourth donor makes a term-of-years pledge with no ultimate commitment.

Finally, the fifth donor does not give at all because she needs the income. The sixth donor gives a value of stock he is secure with that is probably not at our gift level and we miss the upside.

These strategies are not for everyone. Not every agency can handle these funding alternatives. However, the agency that has the needs and pressures of its donors in mind is going to be thinking "out of the box" and therefore be successful.

In all cases, the agency gets the impact of a $100,000 gift as an outright gift which can be used for its project either directly as funding or as an endowment. These examples all provided the donors maximum flexibility in making their distribution of the $100,000.

By these examples we can see that as we think about our opportunities, it may pay dividends to get "out of the box" and look in. Your donor may have a gift for you.

Practice Your ABCs

Cultivate Donors for Successful Solicitation of Gifts

Jack North has a net worth of more than $1 million. For several years, he had been a member of a respected organization that we will call the National Association of Children's Issues (NACI). Yet when asked for a $25,000 gift, he turned down the organization.

The fund raiser and the volunteer were stumped. North had the capacity to make the gift. He also had a history of affiliation with the organization, during which he demonstrated his interest.

What went wrong?

Clearly, the element lacking was that there had not been sufficient cultivation of Mr. North by NACI. He lacked the feeling of ownership in NACI that would have created a strong enough relationship for him to make a gift of this size.

All fund-raising professionals know it is necessary to cultivate a donor. But many do not understand what cultivation means or how it can be used. Each person has his or her own way and style of cultivating prospects. The cultivation of a donor should flow naturally. Insincerity will be quickly discovered and harm the relationship.

The following is a sampling of the ways in which one might cultivate a prospective donor. Following the ABC's of cultivation will stimulate the ways and means by which relationships can emerge, thus allowing significant gifts to follow.

A APPRECIATION. The acknowledgment of a donor's worth — not his or her economic worth — but his or her worth to the organization in view of time and talent, in addition to treasure, is an excellent way to cultivate the donor's interest. Many organizations are now adopting acknowledgment and appreciation policies. The extension of appreciation to a donor might be accomplished through personal notes to the donor, informal recognition of the donor by members of the board of directors, casual mention of the donor in his or her role in various activities, highlighting donor activities in organizational publications and other personal expressions.

B BORROWING. Borrowing from a prospect is a way to develop a relationship on an entirely different level. Some agencies might be able to accomplish this by borrowing a donor's truck to move materials; the use of a lake or summer property for a retreat for staff and board membership; silver service for an important event; possibly even the use of a donor's plane for transportation.

C COUNSELING. Counseling with prospects concerning their impressions, understandings and ideas regarding your nonprofit agency is an effective way to indicate your need for advice in order for the organization to move forward. It would be appropriate, when counseling with a prospect, to find some way to utilize the information the prospect has provided. If there is a need or reason why the counsel of this prospect needs to be cloaked in some level of confidentiality, that adds an additional dimension to the relationship.

D DELIBERATE. Cultivation of a prospect is not something that should be left to chance. You need to be deliberate in your efforts to involve, inform and enlighten your prospect. The key here is to create a sense of spontaneity as well as organization.

E EMPATHY. Building a donor's empathy, understanding and sensitivity to the needs of the institution can be accomplished through the sharing of frustrations, crises and problems, as well as assistance in the solution.

F FEEDBACK. Giving a donor feedback on his or her worth and work with the agency provides an important link between the donor and his or her role. If the donor is interested in the financial standing of the agency, then giving feedback on the finances of the organization on a regular basis can be important. If the donor is interested in the programmatic aspects or legislative activity of the agency — again, feedback. Providing personal and individualized feedback can be valuable.

G GUIDANCE. Each agency needs assistance in its direction. Each prospective board member who has particularly strong expertise in a field, such as the programmatic, financial, construction, retail or other, should be utilized often. As an example, one particular organization has an advisory board that never meets as a group. The advisory board is made up of individuals who have particular expertise in a wide variety of functional areas. When an issue arises for that agency, a call is made directly to the person with the needed skills.

H HOME. Frequently, the activities surrounding the relationship between an agency and the individual prospect take place in the agency's headquarters or office facilities. Finding an opportunity for discussion and meetings in the prospect's home is another way to link the agency. It may be that you would seek the person's home to be volunteered for use in conducting subcommittee meetings, organizational meetings, etc. In addition, the use of the CEO's home for similar meetings brings the prospect closer to the agency.

I INDIVIDUALIZE. Cultivation activities are not lock-step activities. All aspects of cultivation are elements that must be handled on a one-on-one basis or a one-on-few basis. It should not be one in which we do for hundreds of people or even several people, but each should be tailored and individualized.

J JOIN. The prospect should be encouraged, if he or she has not yet joined the appropriate organizations, special-interest groups, action committees, focus groups, etc., to become a part of the organization.

K KINDNESS. The extension of a kindness to a prospect continues to establish value between the donor and the organization. For an elderly prospect, the occasional offer of transportation is appropriate. For a vital volunteer, the offer of availability to find a substitute when the volunteer must tend to other responsibilities. For the donor, when financial trends turn downward to demonstrate an ongoing support for the success of the donor. All of these and many more produce an appropriate extension of kindness.

L LUNCH. The opportunity to take a prospect to lunch and encourage his or her involvement and understanding of the organization is an obvious technique that is used to foster relationships. "When we meet, we eat."

M MONITORING. Providing opportunities to monitor the organization, seeking specific action on the part of the prospect to give his or her feedback as the result of a special assignment to monitor a particular phase of a program or project or element. Assignment as the chair of a special task force also is a welcome gesture.

N NON-CASH GIFTS. Those elements that could be utilized by the agency that do not involve specific cash allocations by the donor can be vital.

O OFFICE. Make sure the donor has an opportunity to work in the agency and be associated with the agency for periods of time in which feedback is offered on their work.

P PATIENCE. The process of cultivation is not accomplished in a short period of time. When it is accomplished effectively, it occurs over a long period of relationship building and developing. Boards and executives need to be patient in the development of those relationships. These strong relationships will yield invaluable economic rewards.

Q QUALITY. You may find that at times you want to provide gifts to the donor for a particular occasion, such as birthdays, anniversaries, or others that seem appropriate. It is important that the gifts not be extravagant, but that they be good quality and related to the purpose of the institution, such as emblems of the organization. The Girl Scouts sometimes give variety packs of cookies or something made by the children, and many other examples could be cited.

R RELATIVES. There are many occasions in which donor prospects can be cultivated by involving members of the donor prospect's family — immediate or extended. Seek opportunities to get to know other family members. Honor those family members and communicate with them.

S SELECTIVITY. In all activities dealing with cultivation, the donor should sense and understand that you have been very selective in making the requests, asking for involvement. Seeking the advice of this prospect is valuable in consummating the cultivation relationship.

T TIMING. Donor prospects do not have the same agenda that you do in trying to reach the point of a gift. They have their own personal business activities that will interfere with your "fast-track" cultivation strategy. Be sensitive to the timing of the donor. On the other hand, do not deliberately delay the prospecting activity.

U UNRELATED ACKNOWLEDGEMENT. If you know from discussions that the donor prospect is interested in model trains, oil paintings, bridge, automobiles, it would be appropriate in your travels and readings to find something that relates to and would be unique to that donor prospect and send it with a note acknowledging his or her interest. Appreciation of these unrelated interests will be influential.

V VICTORY. With every nonprofit organization, there are opportunities to celebrate. Victory is not only a sign of the success of the annual fund or capital fund drive. It can be likened to the success that a child has when he or she begins to function more independently. Be alert to these opportunities. Allowing the donor prospect to participate in these victories is vital.

W WORTH. This important motivator for a prospect will encourage greater ownership by the donor prospect to move further down the road to success. Each individual wants to feel his or her involvement has had a measure of worth. We should encourage those activities that demonstrate worth.

X XAVIER, KANSAS. Know the family roots of your prospect. Where did he or she grow up? Was it a small town in Kansas or a large city in California? What connections do you have to those origins? How does the prospect feel about his or her past? Where is the family now? Your desire to know the prospect thoroughly will be appreciated and valued.

Y YEARLY UPDATE. It's good policy to annually review — perhaps on the birthday of the prospect — the cultivation strategy for that particular prospect. What has worked well? What new strategies should be implemented?

Z ZEAL. A prospect should see the energy for the nonprofit in the work of all staff members. This zeal for their mission will be contagious and encourage the donor to reach for the best opportunities to make a difference.

Seldom has a prospect ever reported that they have been over cultivated. While some may not encourage particular cultivation activity because they feel the donor is not interested or cares, remember the donor always has the opportunity to say no. Sincere, reasonable and serious efforts to cultivate will be taken in good faith. The link of cultivation following identification of the donor can effectively result in the closing of a significant gift.

30 Commandments for Successful Fund Raising

Fund raising is an opportunity to implement important projects or ideals through the activation of a donor's gift. Fund raising is a means to an end, but not an end in itself.

To ensure you are successful in the development of a donor relationship and the eventual solicitation, you must take a proactive approach. The following rules are designed to encourage you to heighten your knowledge and understanding of the fund-raising process as well as reinforce your values as a fund raiser. These items may introduce new ideas or simply reinforce what you already know.

1. ***Believe in yourself and your institution.*** If you do not appreciate yourself, your institution and the reason for raising funds, you will not be successful.

2. ***Maintain a positive attitude.*** Success depends on your ability to communicate a positive attitude in every area of your work.

3. Develop a plan with achievable goals. An unrealistic goal is merely a dream.

4. Learn one new strategy every day. Listen to your donors, watch other fund raisers and, each day, try to develop one new idea that will enhance your fund-raising abilities.

5. Use your automobile as a learning center. There are several audio tapes available on successful fund-raising strategies. Use them instead of listening to the radio.

6. Focus on current donors as often as possible. These individuals already believe in your institution and typically have not yet given to their capacity.

7. Shake hands firmly. No one wants to shake hands with a dead fish.

8. Don't prejudge your prospects. There may be a number of individuals who may not look like good donors, but may very well be.

9. Understand your donors' needs. Question and listen to your donors. Visit with them about their needs and why they are a part of your organization. Take notes as the prospects are talking in order to indicate the importance of their comments.

10. Listen with the intention to understand. Listening is not just "not talking." Try to comprehend and feed back to your prospect what you heard them say.

11. Establish long-term relationships. Donors are individuals who appreciate and value our institutions. Build on those relationships.

12. Be prepared. Knowing yourself, your agency and its projects is critical to your ability to be successful. Know your prospects' businesses and industries. Understand your prospects before you make the call.

Read the business and trade journals of your best prospects. It is best if you understand and appreciate the world in which they operate so you can more effectively communicate.

13. **Become a resource for your prospects.** As you travel and communicate with others, you will learn a lot about a number of businesses. If there is an idea or article that relates to one of your prospects, clip it and send it to them.

14. **Always look professional.** Your appearance reflects not only on you, but on your agency.

15. **Be prompt.** Lateness is never respected.

16. **Use humor.** Humor is our greatest tool in fund raising. Laughing signals approval; therefore, it is important to get the donors laughing.

17. **Use questions.** Encourage your donor to ask about your projects and then respond appropriately.

18. **Use testimonials to overcome objections.** Sharing other success stories will make the donor feel more at ease and more important.

19. **Anticipate objections.** Be prepared to respond to the traditional objections. Know the difference between a stall and a real objection.

20. **Tell the truth.** You will never have trouble remembering what was said if you always tell the truth.

21. **Do not put down the competition.** Remember the old adage — if you cannot say something nice about someone, don't say anything at all.

22. **Ask for the gift.** This sounds simplistic, but many times this step is neglected or assumed.

23. *After asking for the gift, be quiet.* This should be the golden rule of fund raising and should be adhered to at all times. If your donors say no, ask them why and listen objectively to their response.

24. *Deliver more than the donor expects.* Treat each donor as if he or she were the most important person to the success of your institution. Satisfy your donor's complaints in less then 24 hours.

25. *Don't blame others when the fault is yours.* It is poor form. Taking responsibility for your actions is appreciated and valued by others.

26. *Evaluate yourself every month.* Think of your review in terms of presentation, goal achievement, education and general attitude.

27. *Make it easy.* Give your donor the easiest way to make a gift.

28. *Elicit unsolicited referrals on a regular basis.* Ask about others who might need or desire our involvement.

29. *Be memorable in a professional way.* Become competent at everything you do. Find mentors and use them. Hang around successful people. Realize that the biggest obstacle to your success as a fund raiser is yourself.

30. *Have fun.* If you enjoy what you do, everyone will want to be a part of your team.

These suggestions can assist you in developing a strong pattern of personal success, as well as philanthropic support for your institution. We in philanthropy have the opportunity to be a part of the greatest enabling profession that exists. Our work may be limited to a specific area, but our impact can be very broad.

Chapter 4:

Who to Ask

Frequently, I become frustrated when I listen to fund raisers voluntarily limit their prospect pool. One major principle I have worked by is that **everyone** is a prospect. It can be very hard to imagine the wealth of some who might be close to your organization. Don't leave it to the imagination. With so much wealth in this country, it would be easy to overlook a significant philanthropist.

The best-selling book, *The Millionaire Next Door*, is featured in a special essay, "15 Fund Raising Opportunities with The Millionaire Next Door." The authors of the book, whom I have followed for many years, are experts in matters of the affluent.

Two articles, "Research, Research, Research," and "Prospect Research: Know Thy Flock" focus on the necessity of having more than a general knowledge of your prospects. "Research, Research Research," parallels the real estate axiom of location and points to the depth of knowledge necessary for a successful solicitation. "Prospect Research: Know Thy Flock" reminds us to look first at those closest to us.

With proper research and knowledge of your prospective donor, you can close a gift with someone you now don't know.

"How to Ask for the Next Gift After Being Turned Down" gives clues on how to get back to closing your gifts after a disappointment.

15 Fund-Raising Opportunities with The Millionaire Next Door

Harold lived in a $40,000 home.
Dick was a government highway engineer.
George sold manufactured products.
Oliver made lubricating pumps.
Marguerite owned a couple of Dairy Queens.
Georgia was a banker.

These men and women all are illustrations of the people identified in the best selling book, *The Millionaire Next Door*. This book, by Thomas J. Stanley and William D. Danko, identifies the characteristics of individuals in this country who have accumulated wealth to the million-dollar level.

It is estimated that there will be 5,625,000 millionaires by the year 2005.

Are you ready to seek gifts from the millionaires living near you? One of the keys to successful philanthropic efforts is the ability to identify donors who fit this category and who, ultimately, can be brought to realize the impact their wealth can have in changing people's lives.

These 15 opportunities result from the analysis of Stanley and Danko:

1. *Recognize that there are people who are millionaires who may be living right next door.* This may sound obvious. There are more millionaires today than ever before, and more being created every day. You cannot find them or seek them out unless you acknowledge their presence. However, we all have a tendency to look for somebody else's donor. How many times have we been sitting in a donor identification meeting listening to someone else say, "I noticed that Georgia made a gift to the children's home," or "It was interesting to see the level of gift Bill gave to that hospital."

By contrast, how often do we really work at identifying our donors, how they relate to our organization; and — in this context — do they fit any of the qualifications of a millionaire next door?

2. *Twenty percent of the millionaires are retired.* Frequently, when people say they are retired, we immediately believe that they are on a fixed income and are unable to make the level of gifts they were able to make during their careers.

In response to this stereotype, recent studies have identified three types of retirees, of which the retired elite is a qualified candidate for fund raising. The retired elite represent almost one-third of those retired.

As an example, Mr. Richard Spencer spent most of his life as a manufacturer's representative, traveling many states. He was a good steward of his resources and lived in a frugal environment. He and his wife, who was a piano instructor, loved the local community college. Prior to Mr. Spencer's death, the couple made a $1 million outright gift and a $2 million gift to the college through their estate. Their gift created a marvelous concert hall — Spencer Hall.

Were the Spencers on anyone's list? No, he was a retired salesman and she was a piano teacher. Yet the Spencers certainly were millionaires; and moreover, the College found a common ground to seek a gift.

3. **Two-thirds of the millionaires next door are self-employed.** Do not be fooled by an income evaluation of wealth. The men and women who constitute this group of philanthropists have made their wealth because:

> *they want control of their own destinies;*
> *they want to solve problems;*
> *they want to be the CEOs of their organizations;*
> *they want no limits on their income;*
> *they are not blinded by money, but are interested in the challenge of developing the business.*

These millionaires will need very specific creative strategies for giving. One successful strategy with this group is a pledge over a period of years in which they are able to set the "timing" of the pledge payment. This strategy responds to the issue of control, and also provides an avenue for them to assist your organization in solving problems — which fulfills their needs for a challenge.

Norbert Maley, who has been in the construction business for many years, constantly used to say to us during our campaign evaluation meetings, "You know, I'm just not sure what the next six months holds for me." For forty years this man has been successful. Finally, I asked him, "Norbert, have you ever been able to project out more than six months?" He looked at me with amazement and said, "No, I have never really known what the future holds for me more than six months out." These donors can respond with significant gifts if given a creative opportunity. Self-employed people need strategies for giving that provide them confidence that they are not giving away their futures.

4. *Look for a dull business.* These millionaires frequently work in fields that do not interest white-collar workers.

> *They design, manufacture, and distribute lubricating pumps.*
> *They are in the trash business.*
> *They have developed paint formulas.*
> *They sell Dairy Queen.*
> *They build a company that lets people rent before they buy.*
> *They own a short-line railroad.*

These are just examples of businesses that are owned by millionaires who have come to philanthropy.

All of these businesses and careers are interesting to the person who owns the business, but are seen by many as dull businesses. They are not involved in the stock market as their main means of income, they are not involved in sports or show business; but yet they are able to provide important philanthropic dollars as a result.

An example: a man who developed a short-line railroad company provided the funds to build a community center in a small Kansas community.

5. *While the average millionaire next door is in his mid-50s, for philanthropic purposes, we want to focus on him when he is 60 or older.* First, it is important to note that, according to studies, most millionaires are men and, obviously, relatively young. The important realization for fund raisers is that ultimately most wealth flows through the hands of a woman. While the wealth may be held presently by the male, it is important to begin cultivation of both the male and female since, ultimately, it is anticipated that the female will be in charge of the gift.

Secondly, we must review our constituent base for males who, ten years ago, were in their mid-50s and may have qualified as millionaires next door. These men probably are beginning to consider the possibility of leaving a legacy. We need to be prepared to suggest to these prospects creative methods of transferring their wealth to the next generation.

An example of such a transformation is in the case of the Apples. The Apples generated significant wealth during their lives through a variety of businesses. They owned a tree farm and wanted to make a gift to their church building drive. It was suggested that they transfer and/or trade the tree farm for a series of office buildings that could provide appropriate income as a part of lead trust.

The resulting transfer of $1 million in assets to an office facility now provides a $100,000 annual distribution to their church. After the lead trust is completed, in ten years, the office facility goes to their grandchildren and provides an opportunity to leave a legacy and to pass important dollars to the next generation.

6. *Taxable income of $131,000 represents seven percent of wealth.* A few years ago, a Southwestern Bell employee of more than 40 years retired. He had supported and invested in the two things he knew best — AT&T and Southwestern Bell. At the time of his retirement, he expressed that as a result of installing

phones in more than 30,000 homes during his career, he was able to witness first-hand the freedom and flexibility that seeing-eye dogs provided to the blind. On that day, he made a gift of more than $1 million to the Seeing Eye Dog Foundation of Illinois.

This Southwestern Bell employee had a relatively small annual income, but had worked and preserved his wealth. Certainly, he qualified as a millionaire.

7. ***Average net worth of $3.7 million, with six percent of the millionaires having wealth over $10 million.*** This factor is important to consider because gifts made by these donors do not have to be outright gifts. We must review and seek planned-gift components that are compatible with current gift-income opportunities. Also, it is important to recognize that this average net worth is for individuals in their mid-50s. By the time they decide to become philanthropic, their net worths will have grown significantly. The following states will have the estimated highest average estate level in the year 2000:

Utah	$4.7 million
DC	4.7 million
Indiana	4.2 million
Florida	3.8 million
Virginia	3.4 million
Louisiana	3.2 million
Missouri	3.2 million
Texas	3.2 million
Hawaii	3.1 million
Oklahoma	3.0 million
Washington	3.0 million
Pennsylvania	3.0 million

By the year 2000, there will be 66,177 deaths of millionaires. Of their wealth, $24.65 billion will go to taxes, $64.17 billion will go to spouses, $14.12 billion will go to charity and $36.07 billion will go through some type of life-time transfer.

While $14.12 billion will go to charity in this first distribution, remember there is opportunity for philanthropy in the $64.17 billion transferred to a spouse and the $36.07 billion transferred to others.

8. ***Ninety-seven percent of millionaires are homeowners who have lived in their homes for 20 years or more.*** It is beneficial to always research property owners near and around your organization. I am reminded of the wonderful gift by Harold Norris to a home for children with disabilities. He lived in a modest home near the children's home and only had been a modest contributor. However, following the death of his wife, he made a gift of $597,000 because he and his wife always enjoyed the children's trick-or-treating and Christmas caroling.

9. ***Eighty percent of the millionaires are first-generation wealth.*** Frequently, it is assumed that those who have wealth must have inherited money. Businesses that have the highest profitability are:

Coal mining
Physicians
Osteopathic physicians
Dentists
Optometrists
Bowling alleys
Chiropractors
Drug stores
Veterinarians
Legal services

Have you researched the people who perform these services or own these businesses in your area?

10. *Most millionaires live well below their means.*
Their cars, clothes, homes, jewelry or lack thereof
may not necessarily fit your expectations of
millionaires. In fact, a trust officer quoted in the
book said, "We do not define wealthy, affluent or
rich in terms of material possessions. Many people
who display high consumption lifestyles have little
or no investments, income producing assets,
common stocks, bonds, private businesses, oil and
gas rights, timber or land." Most people who live in
upscale neighborhoods have little real wealth.

Favorite cars of the millionaire next door.

Ford	10.0%
Cadillacs	9.0%
Lincoln	8.0%
Jeeps, Lexus & Mercedes	6.5%
Oldsmobile	6.0%
Chevrolet	5.6%
Toyota	5.0%
Buick	4.3%
Nissan and Volvo	2.9%
Chrysler and Jaguar	2.7%

Only 6.2 percent of the millionaires hold any type
of platinum credit card. Frugal is how they would
describe themselves.

11. *The millionaire next door is well educated.* More
than 80 percent of millionaires are college graduates.
Certainly, as we consider this particular prospect, we
need to think in terms of individuals who have
valued and utilized their educations.

**12. *While only 17 percent of the millionaires attended
private schools, more than 55 percent of their
children go to private schools.*** The key element here

is to study carefully the names of children who attend private schools and the list of parents and grandparents paying the fees. In many cases, these represent our new millionaires.

13. ***The new millionaires invest 20 percent of their income annually.*** Obviously, this makes them a better deferred-gift prospect as they look to the future. It is expected that, in the year 2000, nearly 65,000 millionaire estates will exist, valued at $193 billion.

14. ***The millionaires characterize themselves as tightwads.*** While interviewing for the book, interviewees were asked if they would like to have $200 to $250 donated to their favorite charity. Invariably, the response was, "I am my favorite charity." It is important to develop ways to best understand and appreciate this important position and way of thinking.

15. ***The millionaires next door, when reaching the age of 60, will want to leave a legacy.*** We must be prepared to help them develop that legacy.

These 15 opportunities, used separately or together, could be key in the identification, cultivation and solicitation of your millionaires.

Know your prospect and be strategic in your cultivation of the prospect. You can close these gifts if you pay attention to the donor's needs.

Prospect Research
Know Thy Flock

Today, the field of prospect research is the most challenging area of interest for fund-raising professionals. Philanthropists desire to have a significant impact on their chosen institutions. It seems the number of individuals supporting causes is diminishing. But at the same time, the opportunities for substantial gifts are increasing.

In the field of prospect research, particularly with regard to significant gifts, it is not unusual for fund raisers to overlook the most obvious prospect base. This demonstrates a lack of real knowledge of those closest to their institutions.

Following are four steps toward understanding and appreciating your current prospect base.

1. ***Current and past employees.*** Most professionals in the nonprofit arena at times are involved in soliciting gifts from current and past employees. Many of these individuals make severe economic sacrifices to work in those institutions. Yet, occasionally there are individuals who —because of personal family circumstances, have chosen lifestyles or made a decision not to marry and have a family — are able to accumulate reasonable sums of wealth that would be

available for potential distribution either as a current gift or as an estate and planned gift.

In order to pursue this avenue, it is important to understand and appreciate current and past employees. Past employees should be acknowledged, recognized and included regularly in information and activities of the organization. This is especially significant if they are individuals who have been with the institution for many years and have retired with the institution.

For example: You might find a former executive director of a Girl Scout operation who may have never had children and may have acquired fairly substantial resources during her life through pensions and other lifestyle decisions. Those funds potentially are available, because no one knows and understands better than she the importance of Girl Scouting.

2. *Past and Current Board Members.* Without exception, pursue cultivation of current and past members of your board of directors. Frequently, not enough is known about these persons to develop an appropriate solicitation. One director of development, when asked about a member of his board, responded, "Well, I think he's a gambler." Professional research revealed that he was a stockbroker (which may have certain gambling connotations, but is far removed from being considered a gambler). Further, the individual had substantial resources available.

Each member of the board, current and past, should be interviewed by the director of development and executive director of the institution in order to gain information in these three areas.

- ■ What is each individual's current business and why is it successful?

- Ask about the person's family and heritage, including where he or she grew up and what business the family was involved in.

- Ask the person to describe his or her current immediate family. Are there children? Are they successful? Married? Divorced? Widowed?

The answers to these questions can provide good threshold information regarding the viability of current and past board members as potential prospects for substantial gifts.

3. **Volunteers.** Frequently, volunteers are active within institutions who provide support through the use of their time. Many of those individuals know our organizations inside and out. There is opportunity for us to find gifts among those individuals.

It is interesting to discover why someone with no children would volunteer to serve as a receptionist for Ronald McDonald House. What draws that person to the House? Individuals who fit a category, either because of inheritance, lifestyle or decision not to have family, may have acquired resources that could be available either through outright or deferred means.

Again, the director of development and executive director of the institution should have a standard procedure of interviewing and evaluating volunteers and reviewing their background in order to gain information in these three areas.

- What motivates the person to be a volunteer with the institution?

- Ask about his or her family and heritage, including where the person grew up and what business the family was involved in.

■ Ask about the person's current immediate family. Are there children? Are they successful? Married? Divorced? Widowed?

Frequently, these interviews can be utilized as profiles. One last recommendation: Each volunteer profile should include a photograph so they can be visually identified.

4. *Neighbors.* Frequently, nonprofit institutions are located in residential areas. Knowledge and appreciation of the neighbors who have provided an insulated support for your operations sometimes can yield substantial benefit. It is critical to know and understand who owns property and is living in the community surrounding your institution. A periodic, possibly annual, neighborhood appreciation evening can be an important opportunity to yield potential new prospects for fund raising.

As a result of expressing gratitude for their indulgence of your institution in their neighborhood, you are able to convey a sensitivity and appreciation of the sacrifice they may have to make at times for your institution's location. This type of activity certainly was beneficial to a foundation for crippled children. A neighbor who appreciated the children caroling at Christmas time and trick-or-treating at Halloween made a gift of $597,000 to finish the foundation's capital campaign. He had never even set foot inside the institution.

These four avenues, when exercised, can substantially broaden and deepen the strength of the prospect pool for most nonprofit institutions. Express to employees, board members and volunteers your interest in them as individuals and your interest as to why they support the institution. This can yield substantial resources. Their connections, relationships and strength of commitment can be critical to any long-term fund-raising successes.

So, before you begin searching for the "big hitter" in town, stop and look inward for your best prospects. They are closer than you think.

In one college's capital campaign, more than $4 million was committed by members of the retired faculty. In a social-service institution, members of the volunteer community assembled several $100,000 gifts. Those gifts demonstrate how commitment causes donors to dig deep. Your job is simply to know them, appreciate them and encourage them to cross the bridge from wanting to do the right thing to doing it. And that distance is closer than you think.

How to Ask for the Next Gift After Being Turned Down

People frequently tell me that I must love rejection to be in the fund-raising business. The truth is, I hate rejection as much as anyone and I avoid it as much as possible. Obviously, however, once in a while it happens.

The best way to handle it is to make another ask and close another gift. That ask must come from the self-confidence and security that thorough preparation can provide.

Self confidence is not an all-or-nothing personality trait. It is not something you either have or don't. The following five strategies will help you prepare as you close your next gift with confidence.

1. *Examine what you did wrong in the last solicitation.* It has been said that only those who do nothing, do nothing wrong. If you made a mistake, recognize it and let it go. Learn from it and move on.

2. *Look for the progress you did make in your last solicitation and reward yourself with a treat.*

Knowing how to relieve pressure on yourself is as important as knowing how to put it on. Give yourself a break.

3. ***Develop several strategies for overcoming objections on your next ask.*** You may want to draft two or three entirely different solicitations for the same ask.

4. ***Practice it out loud.*** Conduct this solicitation as if you were totally confident of success. Behave "as if" you are going to be victorious. You will be surprised how it gives you confidence.

5. ***Be mentally and emotionally prepared for your presentation.*** Preparation should put you "on top of your game." Work your success "out of the box." Be flexible and stay relaxed. Look for alternative ways to find success. Those anticipated setbacks usually are not there.

Finally, your self confidence will provide you a reward if you incorporate these five strategies and work them over and over again. Self confidence about your ability to succeed will come not only from practice, but will build with each succeeding success.

Research, Research, Research

We've all heard the three rules for selling real estate: Location, Location, and Location. Similarly, there are three rules for successful fund raising: Research, Research and Research. Proper donor identification depends on a thorough understanding of an individual's giving capacity, interests, concern for your organization, and personality. Without research, you are reduced to relying on guesswork and luck.

Universities began to focus on research in the eighties, when full-time researchers took responsibility for major-gift solicitations. This investment paid off for many institutions.

Out of those successes come these recommendations:

1. ***Create a development committee to discuss prospective donors.*** The committee should help the research office gather as much information as possible about the prospect's interests and giving capacity.

2. ***Mail targeted surveys directly to alumni, constituents and friends.*** We found that these prospects were often willing to volunteer information about interests, visions, and even personal finances.

3. ***Discuss money with prospective major donors.*** The management of financial resources is a familiar and important subject to most wealthy individuals. Such discussions are not only appropriate, but expected and even appreciated.

4. ***Record everything related to prospective donors, including their giving capacities and interest in making gifts.*** Recording this information in a simple computerized database is absolutely essential.

5. ***Don't try to research all your prospects.*** Limit your research based on the size of your staff and your ability to do a thorough job. University databases hold thousands of names, but not more than two percent are part of the ongoing, dynamic major-gift prospect list.

6. ***Use the "common sense test" before making a solicitation.*** Research is valuable, but it is not an exact science. As you review each name on your research list, ask yourself if it makes sense to solicit this person for a major gift. Ask someone close to the prospect. Remember, too, that some of the best background information comes from the donors themselves. People enjoy discussing their successes and setbacks, and their relationship with your institution.

Your research may tell you this prospect is not a prospect. As a result, no gift. On the other hand, you may find that a gift comes in at twice — or ten times — the amount you initially expected, thanks to thorough research.

Chapter 5:

Getting Ready to be Successful

Thorough preparation, humor, exceeding expectations and being strategic are the themes of this chapter.

The first selection, "A Tried and True Strategy" gets down to business — a step-by-step guide to one of the more difficult tasks for many fund raisers — asking for the gift.

Another article highlights a certain element of solicitation that frequently is overlooked: humor. Fund raisers are a serious bunch. However, I have been involved in more successful gift solicitations involving laughter than I have ones that are deep, dark and serious.

That article, "A Light Heart Can Lead to a Heart-Felt Gift" is an excellent way for us to discover those keys to solicitation. Humor usually is best introduced after you know the prospect and know what he or she is like. Humor has a place in philanthropy. Good fund raisers have to have a good sense of humor.

"Success Busters" suggests nine ways in which CEOs and administrators can "kill" the efforts of their fund-raising staffs. Serious attention to the means and type of supervision of fund-raising staff is crucial to closing the gift.

Finally, "Knock 'Em Dead: Exceeding Expectations" is the way to position your donors to win. The question is: How do we prepare ourselves to honestly establish relationships and expectations that create the opportunity to "go the extra mile."

These four articles are linked by the opportunity each suggests to raise your fund raising to a much higher level of sophistication. As a result, you close more gifts.

A Tried and True Strategy

The Solicitation of a Major Gift Prospect Can be Exciting and Satisfying

You have identified your donor. You believe you have cultivated your donor to the point that she is ready, willing and able to make the big gift. You have researched your donor, so you understand her capacity. You believe her interest in your project is high. Now, you must solicit the gift.

How much should you ask for? In soliciting a gift, is it better to have two people than one? Should you send three? Should you invite the donor's spouse? Is it better to meet in her office or at the agency? Should you have a letter or just discuss it? Is it best to ask for a gift range or set a specific gift amount?

These are excellent questions considered by every solicitor at some point in his or her career. Remember that each solicitation of a major-gift prospect should be tailored to the needs and demands of that prospect.

The more the fund raiser tries to develop a single template to apply to all prospects of similar wealth, capacity and interests, the more difficult it is to achieve success.

But there is a blueprint to follow. The following is a tried-and-true strategy on the best way to execute a solicitation of a major-gift prospect.

First, look at the issues. Obviously, the donor has been identified and the capacity of the donor has been researched. You have worked hard to find those areas the donor has in common with your institution. While you have enjoyed the discussions of family trips, meetings and vacations, you also have addressed, during the cultivation period, issues of assets, finance, business standing, etc. You have not been hesitant to ask questions about the success of your donor's enterprise.

The following are activities that need to take place prior to the solicitation of a donor.

1. *Commitment.* You, as the solicitor, have made your own commitment to the capital-funds effort. A donor volunteer should solicit only those individuals who are of similar economic standing. The donor volunteer should have provided a similar level of gift to the one being asked.

Staff members often have the capacity to solicit gifts at a higher level than their own contributions by virtue of their institutional role. However, a personal commitment of some sort has to have been made by staff or volunteer solicitors.

2. *Who's the best person?* The issue is not whether two persons representing the agency are better than three. Rather, it is the identification of whom among your family of volunteers and staff would be the best individual or group to solicit that donor. The selection needs to be done with egos set aside and with the recognition that the goal of the solicitation is to receive the highest-possible gift.

3. *Make an appointment.* It is peculiar how often major gifts are solicited without an appointment. Surprises are rare in the arena of major gifts.

"How do you get an appointment? Won't they just turn you down over the phone?" Getting an appointment should be a reasonably easy task. If you are turned down over the phone, you have not done a sufficient job of cultivating and working with your donor. You are not going to get a gift.

4. *Preparation.* You need to understand your proposal and case for support, and anticipate questions—particularly those issues that may have surfaced with the donor in the past.

5. *Emotional factors.* Consider your own emotional stability on the day of the solicitation. Are you ready to make this solicitation? Do you understand how it will unfold?

6. *Materials.* You need to have all materials necessary for the solicitation. Every solicitation should be conducted orally with a companion letter of proposal outlining very briefly the purpose of the gift, the amount of the gift and any other relevant issues such as recognition.

The Solicitation

Opening. Greet the prospect just as you would for any other occasion. It is important for you, the solicitor, to demonstrate casual confidence as you move forward in the solicitation process.

Questions. Usually, the prospect has several questions on his or her mind. You should decide whether you are going to raise those issues. If you do, you must provide answers. If there is any information you should be bringing back from others as a result of earlier inquiries, you need to bring it to the donor's attention at this time. You should feel that you have done the best possible job in answering all the prospective donor's questions.

Proposal. The proposal should be made orally and in writing. A specific amount should be requested. The issue of whether to place a dollar amount on a proposal frequently arises. Some believe that suggesting a range is appropriate, i.e. $5,000 to $10,000. Some believe you should not ask for a specific gift amount. Some believe in carrying multiple envelopes to the meeting and making the decision during the solicitation. The reality is that if you have schooled yourself well on this prospect, developed your relationship appropriately and understand and appreciate the economic standing of the prospect, then "seat-of-the-pants" adjustments to the strategy during the solicitation are inappropriate. You should determine a specific dollar amount and request that gift.

Once the solicitation has taken place — *"Jane Doe, we would like your support of our project with a gift of $10,000 payable at the rate of $2,000 per year over the next five years"* — Stop Talking! Hand your prospect the letter, invite her to read it, but do not say anything more. Do not say things such as, *"We'll appreciate any size gift you can make,"* or, *"We know these are tough times."*

Closing. There are only three possible answers a donor can give you in regard to a solicitation. The first is "yes." Few have problems understanding what to do with this response.

The second possible answer is "no." You are at a premature time in the solicitation process if you get a "no" without a reasonable explanation.

"No, you may not be aware that I have an institutionalized child." "No, you may not be aware that my

parents have been placed in a nursing home." *"No, you may not be aware that there was a major embezzlement at our firm last year."* Any of these responses represent a "no," but the information received is important and should be made a part of the donor's permanent file. You are then allowed the flexibility to go back to the donor once the issue has been resolved or you have appropriately taken the issue into account in your solicitation.

The third response is "maybe." "Maybe" may mean the donor must contact her spouse, children, parents, a committee, board, trust officer, CPA, attorney, insurance representative, etc. A myriad of individuals may "need to be contacted" before the solicitation can be finalized. You should offer to participate in the presentation of the proposal to those interested parties.

The final element is that you remain in control of the solicitation. You might say to the donor, *"I appreciate your need to meet with others. Can I call you in three days?"* Remember, if you allow the donor to control the next contact, the donor has taken control of the solicitation and you will find it very difficult to decide when it is appropriate to call back.

The solicitation of a major gift prospect can be an exciting and satisfying activity if done correctly, and in a timely and appropriate manner. The outcome should be a predictable win-win scenario. You have accomplished your goals, and your donor may for the first time be enjoying the satisfaction of seeing his/her success support a larger good.

A Light Heart Can Lead to a Heart-Felt Gift

Don't try to be a comedian. Comedy and humor should be strategically used in fund raising. Humor usually is best introduced once you know the prospect and you know what he or she is like.

Because I rarely remember a story, I seldom repeat a story or joke. But I do observe human behavior and I frequently reflect on what is going on in my life. Each of us has to discover his or her own style for humor.

In my life, I waited until after 40 years of age to have a child. Of course, I am proud of him. Naturally, "kids do say the darnedest things." I always mention during my initial few meetings with a client that my son, Austin, is 9 years of age and is a great guy.

For example, one recent Christmas his cousin, Ian, told everyone at the holiday dinner that when he grows up he wants to work for Uncle Bob (that's me!). Austin said nothing at the time. However, on the way home he announced out of nowhere, "Dad, if I can't get a job working for anyone else, I am going to work for you."

This story gives me an opportunity to share with my prospect how important my child is to me and consequently how important the future is for the agency or institution I represent. Clearly, having a quality world is necessary for the future. Virtually all the agencies with which we work have future needs that allow them to make positive changes in the world.

As you see, I'm not looking for humor to create a big laugh — a smile is all I seek. Let's look at several ways you can interject a smile into your cultivation and relationship building in fund raising.

1. ***Know who you are talking with.*** Are they conservative or liberal? What do you have in common? What are their interests? Once, I asked a representative of one of our new clients, which was a Mennonite college, if there was anything about the church precepts that I should be aware of to avoid a faux pas in casual conversation. The president thought a minute and said (this was during the Gulf War), "Don't say, 'Wow, did we really blow up the Iraquis last night!'"

2. ***Make sure your humor references have a local or personalized angle.*** We all want to be a part of the story — not an audience for the story. Tailor your humorous anecdote to seem like it just happened yesterday. Mark Twain once observed, "The best improvisation is rehearsed for 48 hours." Your prospects want to relate to you as much as you want to relate to them.

3. ***Be yourself.*** Anyone can tell a joke. Instead, find your comic persona. What type of humor are you most comfortable with? Some are better at one-liners, some at observational humor, some like story-telling. Timing is everything. Stay close to who you are — you will be most successful.

4. ***There are many ways to speak with humor.*** Enhance your stories, make enlargements to make your point. You are only limited by your imagination.

5. *Humor can be key to keeping the relationship going.* Your job always is to listen and input information. Humor helps maintain and extend a relationship.

6. *The final tip is to enjoy yourself.* Fund raising is serious work, but we will benefit by not taking ourselves too seriously.

Humor has a place in philanthropy. Good fund raisers have to have a good sense of humor. Sharing yourself with your prospect and allowing the prospect to be a part of your life through humor can go along way to cementing the relationship and leading to a gift.

Success Busters

Most CEOs of nonprofit institutions understand that fund raising is a part of their job. However, frequently they retain fund-raising staff to implement the agency's fund-raising objectives.

Henry Ellis is the new director of development at A Very Important Agency (AVIA). He is charged with raising $100,000 a year. After one year, his results were short of expectations. Would he have been more successful if his CEO had given him the kind of support that has been motivating and encouraging? This nine-point test might help answer that question.

Typically, CEOs are attracted to nonprofits, not because of the opportunity to raise money, but the opportunity to have an impact on the projects and programs of those agencies and, therefore, their communities. As a result, many CEOs are not skilled at supervising the uniquenesses of a fund-raising staff.

The following nine "success busters" describe ways in which CEOs and administrators can "kill" the efforts of their fund-raising staff to close gifts.

As you read these items, make note of those that you use in supervising fund-raising staff.

1. Don't listen to the fund raiser's view of projects that have been derived from a donor's perspective. Certainly, CEOs can limit their fund raisers' abilities to be successful if they always reject the fund raisers' understanding of the donors' needs related to the project.

2. ***Don't set specific fund-raising goals or seek a fund raiser's involvement in setting goals.*** All too often, fund-raising goals are set by the money needed to meet the budget at the end of the year. By not involving the fund raiser or understanding how and why the goal has been established, you diminish the creativity the fund raiser can bring in being able to cast the fund-raising needs in an appropriate manner. Additionally, you lose the involvement and ownership of the fund-raising staff members, and lessen their ability to characterize appropriately the institution's needs.

3. ***Don't hire smart people.*** A successful fund raiser frequently is very close to the donors who invest highly in the agency. This can cause anxiety for the CEO and, as a result, they shy away from hiring anyone who is curious, challenging or engaging.

4. ***"Kill" any and all new ideas.*** There are a lot of ideas on ways in which projects can be organized to merge with successful fund raising. One such idea is to take those items within an annual budget that have some appeal to donors, and see if they can be characterized specifically.

5. ***If a new idea does surface, the CEO demands immediate documentation and cost estimates as well as letting the staff member know his or her job is on the line if the new idea does not pan out.*** Obviously, creativity cannot emerge from anybody, including the fund raiser, if this attitude prevails.

6. ***Create a suggestion box, but don't acknowledge or provide feedback to the staff who participate.*** Ask

and accept suggestions, but never let anyone know that those suggestions have any value.

7. *Never question your style of management.* Never look at ways in which you can more effectively facilitate for the fund raiser.

8. *Don't discuss the reasons for projects — just demand funds.* It is very difficult for fund raisers to be successful in closing gifts if they do not understand the need and demand for the gift.

9. *Don't credit the fund raiser with the renewal of current donors; instead always demand new gifts from new donors.* A gift that is renewed is a wonderful gift because it builds a strong, long-term relationship. Of course, new gifts always are needed, but one way to assure that your fund raiser is not going to be successful is to only have them cultivate new donors.

Now it's time to test yourself.

Fund raising is an important part of the success of any nonprofit institution. Serious attention to the means and type of supervision of the fund-raising staff can be critical to success. An internal operational audit can reveal the significance of any deficiency. Philanthropy can and must play a vital role in the success of important nonprofit entities.

It is important to your personal success as CEO that you assess your performance objectively. If you are implementing eight or nine of the failings above, you probably are not very successful in your fund-raising endeavors.

If you exhibit five to seven of the above issues, you have not totally eliminated your fund raisers' opportunity for success; but you have created a number of obstacles to overcome.

If you exhibit only two to four of the items, you could — through only a modest change in your style — increase your fund raisers' capabilities substantially by eliminating those few "killers."

Finally, if you are doing none or only one of these issues, you likely have created a good, positive environment for your fund raiser. Your fund raiser has the opportunity to close many gifts!

Knock 'Em Dead!

Exceeding Expectations

You may have heard of it as "knock-your-socks-off service," "the wow factor," "give them the sizzle," — whatever it is called, it means exceeding your donor's expectations. When you exceed expectations, you are on your way to closing a gift.

The question then is: How do we prepare ourselves to honestly establish relationships and expectations that create the opportunity to "go the extra mile?"

The following 10 strategies can keep you focused on these elements.

1. *Be ready for the donor.* Know your donor. Know his or her background, family, business, relationship to your group, relationship to the community, etc. Be prepared to respond to questions, concerns, problems, obstacles, etc. that may arise.

2. *Be on time, if not early.* It speaks to your respect for the donor when you arrive on time. Arriving early demonstrates that you are prepared to work to meet the donor's needs.

3. *Be persistent.* You may not get the response you desire the first time you meet with this prospect. Your commitment to reaching the prospect will be respected.

4. *Be professional in your appearance.* You need to look the part in representing your institution even in today's casual business attire. You can always remove your coat or tie.

5. *Be confident.* You are representing a terrific project. Don't let that fact take a back seat to anything. Build the right relationship, use humor, and listen to your donor. Don't take the project for granted, but speak in terms of the project's being complete.

6. *Do a demonstration.* Remember, a presentation without a demonstration merely is a conversation. The donor wants to see how this project will impact people's lives. Be ready to show your donor exactly how.

7. *Don't waste time.* Being relevant in all your communication — get to the point. No appointment needs to take longer than 20 to 30 minutes unless the donor/prospect wants more time.

8. *Be truthful.* Always tell it like it is — even though it may not be what the donor wants to hear. The donor will value greatly your candor and truthfulness.

9. *Be genuine.* Fake people come off as such. Nobody wants to give money to people who are not sincere and in support of the mission of their project.

10. *Be a "knock 'em dead" person.* All of these skills lead to a person who has confidence, knows their project, is sincere, trustworthy and a good person. Your donors deserve no less.

Ultimately, fund raising is successful because of these 10 elements, which will assist you in exceeding the expectations of your prospect/donor. We all know that until a donor agrees to fund the project, everything else is just conversation. Most often the one who gets the gift is the person who exceeds expectations and "knocks 'em dead."

Chapter 6:

Where it Works

Five fund-raising case histories are offered for your consideration. Closing those gifts using the strategies outlined in this volume were key to all of their success. Fund raising is easy. Either you meet the goal or you don't. If you don't, you lose. If you do, everyone wins. We, as fund raisers, know the importance of our work.

Two articles focus on one institution, Cerebral Palsy Research Foundation (CPRF) because of the development of an annual fund and a capital/endowment campaign. CPRF's annual-fund growth occurred through the creation of a "living endowment" concept. The capital and endowment project raised $25 million, the largest campaign in the history of Kansas social-service nonprofits.

Kansas Special Olympics provided challenges because they proceeded with their campaign after they purchased their building and acquired debt. This took a good capital project into a debt-retirement campaign.

St. Luke's $50 million endowment hospital campaign marked the issues related to health-care fund raising in the environment of significant change. Their success of $59 million raised was one of the largest endowment efforts for a health-care agency.

Finally, the Magic Empire Council of Girl Scouts discovered for a first-time campaign how key volunteers made significant differences.

We could report on many other successes, but the lessons learned from these agencies is that you can close gifts for your institution. New and young, old and stable, experience or novice, or any other combination — if you prepare.

It's Worth a
$5 Million Endowment

The goal for The Cerebral Palsy Research Foundation (CPRF) was to raise $250,000 in unrestricted annual giving. If CPRF could garner and maintain that level of support, effectively they would have developed the equivalent of a $5 million endowment. (A common income distribution level from endowment is 5 percent.)

Historically, CPRF has enjoyed sporadic fund-raising success. Annual fund raising has ranged from $30,000 to $60,000, occasionally moving to $100,000 due to an estate gift.

Hartsook and Associates was retained to provide an audit of their annual-fund activities.

To secure the annual fund, we reviewed the following criteria:

1. **Volunteers.** What were the opportunities for volunteers, and who had already been engaged?

2. **Consistency.** The messages provided by CPRF had varied over the years and the organization needed a consistent message to its donor base.

3. **Preparation for future Board membership.** There was a small pool of individuals who could succeed a Board that, while still relatively young, was reaching a point that successors were needed.

4. **Prospect research.** CPRF did not know much about many of its previous donors.

5. **CEO support.** There was extraordinary CEO support for a strong annual fund.

6. **Board support.** The Board of Directors was anxious to build a broader base.

7. **Impact of organization.** CPRF had become an important resource, but was not as well recognized as it deserved to be.

8. **Recognition and acknowledgement of donors.** While there had been recognition and acknowledgment, there was not a systematic strategy.

9. **Staff Involvement.** Program staff involvement in fund raising had been limited.

Our analysis of the previous five years of giving indicated that, while there had been particular spiking of gifts throughout that five-year period, essentially annual-fund support amounted to an average of $50,000. Based on our findings, it was our recommendation to develop a two-tiered approach to reaching a $250,000 level.

"In the first year, we raised $125,000 in annual fund support, an increase of $75,000. In the second year, we were able to raise $250,000." said Dan Carney, CPRF Board Chair and a co-founder of Pizza Hut.

The following elements were created with members of the CPRF program staff to determine their needs and develop a greater understanding of how gifts would be used.

1. Review the existing budget in order to determine the elements being funded through unrestricted giving that could be separated and characterized to donors as restricted gifts because of a specific impact.

2. Create an Annual Fund Advisory Panel utilizing successful men and women from the business community of Wichita.

3. Broaden the prospect base of CPRF through the relationships and contacts of the members of the Annual Fund Advisory Committee.

4. Prepare well for each solicitation. Make sure each volunteer has strong support for each solicitation and is not just thrown into the community asking for gifts.

5. Report regularly to the Board and Annual Fund Advisory Committee on the success of the annual fund.

6. Provide opportunity for recognition and acknowledgment throughout this process. CPRF recognized its donors through the Unity of Purpose dinner — an annual event with little participation that was broadened to recognize the success of the organization.

7. Build a prospect database to better understand the donors and why they are giving.

8. Ask in the second year for multi-year pledges to allow donor appeal.

9. Create matching gifts and challenge-gift opportunities so the donors know their dollars will be utilized in a broader appeal.

"We found that members of the community were unaware of the role of CPRF." Mike Burrus, President of Multimedia Cablevision and Chair of the Annual Fund said, "Once we were able to explain the role, we found that individuals were ready to step forward, which has resulted in our success."

The above activities and objectives allowed CPRF to grow from an annual fund of $50,000 to now more than $300,000 in only two years. It is important for the agency to continue this program, the stewardship and the involvement of donors so that their success can continue long term.

The Secret of Campaign Success

How Kansas Special Olympics Raised $1.35 Million

Trade secrets are a dime a dozen in today's business arena. In philanthropy, however, the secret to a good campaign is worth its weight in gold. Nonprofits can spend so much time concentrating on how they will reach their goal, they forget who will help get them there. For Kansas Special Olympics (KSO), the secret to raising a million dollars had as much to do with the people as it did the process.

Kansas Special Olympics was founded in 1970 and has a proud history of providing quality year-round sports training, education and athletic competition programs for individuals with mental retardation. Today, governed by a 20 member Board of Directors, full-time individuals on staff, as well as the support of over 20,000 volunteers, KSO is a model organization utilizing the venue of sports to impact the lives of thousands of Kansans; whether athletes, coaches or volunteers, by affecting their personal, emotional, spiritual, educational, physical and psychological development.

Due to the tremendous growth and expansion of KSO during the past 25 years (participation numbers grew from 200 in their first year, to more than 7,416 during the 1993-94 year), the organization outgrew its state corporate/training facility. In 1995, KSO retained Hartsook and Associates to do a campaign assessment for a new education and program center to meet the current and future demands of the organization. On our recommendation, they entered into a $1.35 million capital campaign in November 1995. Twenty months later the "Together We Win" campaign was successfully completed. The campaign's title was synonymous with the way the campaign unfolded, as every person involved with the campaign seemed to understand and appreciate their single role in the collective effort.

Kansas Special Olympics' capital campaign was initiated with three major objectives:

1. Paying for the facility and renovations

2. Providing for a building maintenance fund for the facility

3. Beginning a paid area director endowment (providing a salary for a person in the field who manages the Special Olympics operations within a geographic designation).

Later in the campaign a fourth objective was added: providing for the technological needs of the organization and its athletes. Upon completion of the campaign, Chris Hahn, President and CEO of KSO says the success of the effort, coupled with the ongoing support the campaign has provided, is better than he had imagined.

"We now have a long-term fund — an endowment that will pay for the building and cover the maintenance expenses that the headquarters office requires," says Hahn. "We have three of our six paid area directors in place, two of which positions are endowed. We've had the opportunity to add some of the most up-to-date technology to our facilities. Plus, we have no mortgage payment on our headquarters facility and its upkeep is paid for by a building endowment maintenance fund. It's a wonderful position to be in," adds Hahn.

Of course, as with any campaign, KSO encountered several surprises (good and bad) along the way. One of the first unexpected obstacles the organization encountered was the effect its choice of a new facility would have on potential donors. Because of an excellent "find" on an existing facility, KSO had purchased their new facility in advance of their campaign kick-off. This was a deterrent in the minds of some potential donors who raised the question "since you're already in a facility, and it's not obviously a financial drain on the organization at this time, where's the urgent need for capital funds?" KSO had to educate these donors in the importance of renovating the new facility, providing for a building maintenance endowment fund, area director endowment fund, and advanced technology funds.

"If I had to do it over again, we would have begun our campaign in advance of buying a building," admits Hahn.

Dale Chaffin, campaign committee chairman and board member for KSO agrees, "The various rules and regulations that foundations have can make a huge difference in your outcome. Whether you already have a building, have bought land, are negotiating, or have a set of plans to build — all make a difference in whether you will receive funds from certain foundations. Every organization has specific rules and regulations, so if any part of your process violates their rules — you're out of the running," says Chaffin. "From the viewpoint of an organization such as ours, their rules don't always make sense. That's where the consulting firm comes in — their key role in the process is to educate the organization. I attended a seminar given by Dr. Hartsook and learned about how the project needed to be executed in an organized and scientific manner. After his firm was retained for the campaign, the guidance in planning, direction during the campaign, and almost as importantly, the pep talks consultant Murray Blackwelder gave us along the way helped us keep focused on our goals and not get discouraged."

Chris Hahn also felt his consultant played a special part in the success of their campaign. "I really appreciated the efforts of Murray to push us and keep us moving through the campaign. He tried to guide, direct, steer and teach us all through the campaign. In a campaign of this magnitude, you spend so much time and focus on the project that you can get overwhelmed and bogged down," says Hahn. "Hartsook and Associates helped give us the support we needed during the campaign, but even more importantly, during the process of the campaign we were taught how to raise funds in larger amounts from corporations and foundations. We now have the skills to be able to do so successfully again in the future."

Ironically, another obstacle KSO faced in soliciting donors stemmed from the fact that it is a "model of efficiency" for Special Olympics nation-wide and nonprofit organizations in general. The goal of KSO is to have a year of operating funds held in reserve, and in early 1998 had approximately two-thirds of their operating funds in reserve. While this was a clear sign of the efficient management of the organization, the size of their reserve account was actually a "questionable" factor in the minds of a few foundations.

"Nonprofits today are in a catch-22. You're expected to manage your organization like a business. If a business makes eight to ten-percent above overhead, they are doing great. For us, that percentage would be the programs we deliver to the athletes. We currently have about 79 cents on the dollar going towards direct program cost, and 21 cents towards administration and development," explains Hahn. "If a business is making 79% profit, they would be high on the hog, yet we get questioned as to whether we are putting enough money into programs. On the other side of the coin, it's just good fiscal management to keep the doors open so you have a good reserve fund — but unfortunately that leads some people to look at it as if you do not need any money."

There were also some very pleasant surprises for KSO along the campaign trail. The organization had anticipated a singular gift in the $150,000+ category and their bread and butter gifts to fall in the $25,000 — $99,000 range. Major gifts actually comprised the majority of their campaign funds with three gifts over $150,000, two gifts over $100,000, and five gifts in the $50,000 — $99,000 range.

KSO's all-volunteer board had 100% participation, with all members making contributions.

Board member Dave Lindstrom, a Burger King franchise owner and former Kansas City Chief football player, was instrumental in getting KSO their lead gift of over $150,000 (the first gift Burger King has ever made of this magnitude). Another board member, John Meara of the CPA firm Meara, King and Company, made tremendous strides for KSO in the Kansas City corporate foundation world. It's unusual to find an organization whose board feels so passionately about what it is doing. KSO is the exception.

Board member John Meara explains why participating in the campaign was so important to him. "Being involved with Special Olympics is one of the most rewarding experiences I've ever had in civic or charitable work, because the organization is made up of people who really care. Everyone involved is contributing their time out of the love of being with Special Olympians. The rewards of being with real people are intangible and irreplaceable. I've been involved with volunteer efforts where you don't feel you're really making any kind of a difference. No one involved with KSO feels that way. Every penny and every hour is being used for the people they serve. KSO is the best run, best organized, best capitalized example of what a state organization should look like," says Meara. "I'm thrilled to have been a part of the successful campaign."

Non-board volunteers echo Meara's praise for KSO. "It was an honor for me to be asked to serve on the fund-raising team — there's no better cause anywhere in the nation as far as individuals are concerned than Special Olympics," says Retired Kansas Attorney General Bob Stephan, an instrumental volunteer.

Members of the organization's vast pool of volunteers made themselves available to go on every call to potential donors and corporations. One campaign committee volunteer, Jim McEnerney, worked with a couple who made a $500,000 cash gift. Another valued gift came when an honorary chairperson was instrumental in getting a $100,000 cash contribution.

The successful completion of KSO's "Together We Win" campaign has not only changed the physical structure of the organization, it has changed the way the organization will raise funds for the future. "Prior to the campaign, we raised our funds through three forms: direct marketing, sponsorship, and special events. Now, and in the future, we will focus on major gift, corporate donations, and deferred giving," says Hahn.

Campaign Chairman Dale Chaffin agrees, "For the long-term, the campaign has helped us have a major focus on endowment giving for the future," says Chaffin. "There's a science to entering into these kinds of campaigns — you have to be educated to the process."

The science of process and the service of people. For Kansas Special Olympics, they're the secret of campaign success.

What We Learned

KSO highlights three elements to successfully closing that gift.

1. ***Know your prospect's rules.*** Plan your actions within their parameters.

2. ***Tension.*** Donors need to appreciate the need for their gifts now.

3. ***Think big.*** Organizations need to be confident of their impact. Donors will respond in kind.

Magic Empire Council of Girl Scouts

Great Empires Aren't Built in a Day

When the Magic Empire Council of Girl Scouts first began to realize its increasing need for capital funds, they knew the fund-raising task rising before them could not be taken lightly. Great empires aren't built in a day. The Council had never undertaken a major fund-raising campaign. Still, Magic Empire's senior management knew that for their organization to continue to accomplish its mission, a great deal of planning and preparation would have to precede any major fund-raising effort.

The Magic Empire Council of Girl Scouts is one of 331 councils chartered by the Girl Scouts of the USA and is charged with administering the Girl Scout program in seven counties in northeastern Oklahoma. It is the largest Girl Scout council in Oklahoma.

The Need Was Evident

Because of tremendous growth within the Council, the need for a new troop camping site became the primary catalyst in what would become the Campaign for Growth, a $3.4 million capital and endowment campaign. From 1989 to 1994, the number of campers attending summer resident camp at Tallchief, the Council's main over-night camp site, grew 94 percent.

"The Girl Scout Council in Tulsa had been extremely successful," explains Ruth Richards, Director of Development for the Council during the campaign, "so the Council had been talking about the dream of a new troop camp for some time. When I came on board, in 1989, we were serving 4,500 girls. By the time I left, in 1997, the Council was serving 7,200 girls. Girls were having to wait three years to get a reservation at camp!"

Concern About Asking For Money From The Community

Although the Council had committed to a concerted effort to raise funds for a new camp in 1989, beginning a campaign was put on hold until things were put in order. "Back in 1990, we began really looking at our group to see where weak spots might be as far as perceptions were concerned," says Bonnie Brewster, Executive Director during the campaign. "As a result of looking at ourselves, we took very important steps to educate our board about a capital campaign and how it should be done right, or not at all."

Since this was the first time the Council would be asking the community for major dollars, they took some deliberate steps to prepare the community for the campaign, including organizing a women's support group and planning a yearly fund-raising event. Those two actions drew in professional women from all over the community, provided a high-profile event at the existing main camp, and began making the first strides toward a capital campaign.

Preparation Necessary

Good preparation was at the heart of the Campaign for Growth. Magic Empire realized the essential importance of taking the time to build a good foundation for their campaign. "You can't just go out and raise $3.4 million," says Brewster. "There are years of preparation." The campaign officially began quietly with a lead gift of $1 million in July of 1994. The Hartsook firm was retained to do an assessment study and as ongoing counsel throughout the campaign.

With a 30-year service record in the Girl Scouts, and 23 years as the Executive Director of Magic Empire Council of Girl Scouts, Brewster's commitment to the campaign cause was rock solid. Her commitment and that of her staff and the volunteer campaign cabinet played a major role in the momentum of the campaign. The campaign cabinet met every two weeks for an hour and a half, for at least a year. "There was an excitement in the air that was contagious," says Brewster. "Ruth Richard's commitment to supporting the structure of the campaign was absolutely critical to our success."

"A lot of spirit and community was established through those meetings," said Richards.

Incredible Leadership

An incredible leadership team who knew the foundation and corporate power structure within the Tulsa community was established in Honorary Chair Jack Zink, a community philanthropist, and Foundation Division Chair Steve Jatras, a retired corporate CEO.

According to Jack Zink, the needs of the Council were concrete enough to demand public attention. "We had a marvelous cause that was evident. Our campaign slogan stated our mission beautifully: 'For over eighty years the

Girl Scout movement has sparked the imagination of small girls and young women and given them a vision for their future: being competent, self-confident adults at ease in an evermore complex world. It is a future that every parent wishes for their daughter.'"

"With such a sincere goal at the heart of the campaign, it was an easy sell to the community," says Zink.

Jack Zink served as an Honorary Co-Chair with his sister, Jill Tarbel, co-trustee with Jack of the Zink Foundation. Also serving as Honorary Chair was the Mayor of Tulsa, and Clydella Hentschell, another civic volunteer. The campaign co-chairs were Janet Zink and Ann Graves, two former Girl Scouts who are prominent Tulsa civic leaders.

Challenge Gifts

Midway through the campaign, upon the firm's recommendation, Magic Empire visited the Kresge Foundation. "We were very excited when we solicited the Kresge Foundation, having no idea what their response would be," recalls Brewster. "To then receive a challenge grant for $350,000 from them was a wonderful statement to the community about the importance of this campaign."

Making the trip to the Kresge office to receive the grant was one of the highlights of the campaign for campaign leaders. "We were treated so wonderfully by the Kresge people, it really made an impact on me," says Jatras, "especially since we were not sure we would receive anything from them."

"One thing that was very unusual for us is that we were required, by the Kresge office, to increase our goal," adds Jatras. "One of their caveats was that a certain amount of funds should be earmarked for ongoing support. We increased our goal, and were able not only to meet that goal, but exceed it and come away with even greater results than we had hoped for originally."

The campaign also received a challenge grant of $500,000 from the Mabee Foundation, a regional foundation which funds many building projects.

Volunteer and Staff Support

Although Magic Empire did not have a board that could easily provide the campaign funds through their own private gifts, the campaign received 100 percent board and staff participation. "The Girl Scout staff was incredible. I was astonished by the amount some of our staff contributed to the campaign, considering their limited incomes," relates Richards, "but that was how important the campaign was to them. They, like everyone involved in the campaign, were giving everything they could for the girls."

Volunteer involvement played an important role in the campaign as the girls' parents and even the girls themselves, raised funds for the campaign. Troop parents raised $50,000. The girls got into the act and raised just under $50,000 with a project called "Coins for Camping". Every troop picked a "thon" (dance-a-thon, bowl-a-thon, walk-a-thon, etc.) and received pledges from neighbors, friends and family. "There was a real sense of ownership in the project, because the girls knew they were helping to build their camp," recalls Brewster.

The success of the girls' campaign is all the more impressive considering the time the event took place. The events were held on their scheduled day, the Saturday after the Oklahoma City bombing. "It was raining horribly and people all over the state were still in shock," recalls Richards, "but the girls still went out and did their best. One troop that held a bounce-a-thon took turns bouncing and making sandwiches for the rescue workers.

I think the girls' commitment illustrated how valuable Girl Scouting is to shaping a girl's attitude toward community service."

The Council also solicited and welcomed volunteer input into what the new facilities would look like, how they would be used, etc., bringing a real sense of unity to the campaign. "Our volunteers are our life-line in scouting," explains Brewster, "asking them to contribute their ideas made them feel like they were an essential part of the process, even if they couldn't contribute financially."

While much of the structure of the Campaign for Growth, Richards "got out of the book," she readily admits she would not have wanted to do the campaign without outside counsel. "The advantage of outside counsel is that of bringing a voice of wisdom into the campaign which carries greater weight than your own. Our counsel served as an enforcer and enthusiast in a way no one else could. Without Hartsook, we would not have gone for the Kresge grant," Richards adds. "We achieved the $3.4 million level because of his involvement."

Bonnie Brewster also gives credit for the campaign success to help from outside counsel. "I believe one of the major reasons we were successful was because of our relationship with outside counsel. Hartsook guided us from the formation of the cabinet and establishing an honorary chair, to how to have cabinet meetings," says Brewster. "Our consultant played a major role in sitting down with our Development Director and strategizing. His input not only increased our credibility, but carried a sense of security through the whole campaign."

Completion On Time and On Budget

The Campaign for Growth wrapped up in just two years with fruits aplenty. The new troop camping site includes a lodge, tent group, tree house, log cabin, covered wagon group, frontier village, central bath houses, storm shelters and site work. Other projects covered under the $3.4 million umbrella included the Tulsa Service Center Conference Wing, safety and program improvements, renovation to existing Tulsa Service Center, and outreach programs in Tulsa's Public Housing Communities.

While new facilities and programs clearly testify to the success of the campaign, the intangible rewards of the effort will serve to strengthen and stabilize the Council for years to come. "The Campaign for Growth has given Magic Empire Council of Girl Scouts confidence," says Richards. "It has allowed them to become much stronger advocates for girls and girl programs, not merely within the confines of scouting, but within the community."

Fund Raising Was Fun

One of the best perks of working on Magic Empire's Campaign for Growth was the sense of "fun" carried throughout the entire effort. It's an element that can only be present when solid preparation, exceptional goals, and an Integrated Campaign™ approach is present.

"We had a great case, great team, great counsel, and a lot of fun," insists Richards. "It all made for a great experience. Even our big fund raisers and campaign chairs told us how much fun they had during the campaign and that's not a usual occurrence!"

"I have a tremendously good feeling about the campaign," concurs Brewster. "We had an opportunity to make something great and we did it well."

What We Learned

Magic Empire Council of Girl Scouts identified several important lessons to closing gifts.

1. *The role of the early gift in giving the project credibility.* The million-dollar pledge sent a message to Tulsa that this was an important effort.

2. *Women as philanthropists.* This project highlighted giving not only for women, but more importantly, by women.

3. *Leadership perks.* The insight and excitement of the Kresge visit will never be forgotten by the campaign leaders (and also major donors).

Strength Amidst Change

St. Luke's Hospital Foundation

At a time when anxiety was high over mergers, buyouts and acquisitions, and what effect they would have on the identity of our hospitals, a Kansas City hospital prepared itself to take the dominant position in determining its future. Thanks to the successful completion of the $59 million Strength Amidst Change campaign, Saint Luke's Hospital of Kansas City, Missouri, is now able to influence the shape of its own destiny.

The goal of the three-year campaign was to raise funds to strengthen and sustain medical education and research at Saint Luke's Hospital, enhancing its stature as a private teaching hospital.

"We were in a unique position in that we saw an opportunity to help determine our own destiny, rather than waiting for the national anxiety over healthcare to determine it," says Harold Schultz, Executive Director at Saint Luke's Hospital Foundation.

The 35-year-old Foundation is the Hospital's philanthropic arm and raises money for medical education and research at Saint Luke's, the largest private teaching college in the Kansas City area. As director of the Strength Amidst Change campaign, Schultz's prime role was major-gift solicitation. With 20 years' expertise in service as a college president, Schultz possessed a great deal of savvy regarding fund raising and led the process with consummate skill.

Setting A Goal

Saint Luke's selected Hartsook and Associates to do an Integrated Campaign™ Assessment in the Fall of '93. The study was completed during the "crisis in healthcare" when a great deal of anxiety existed among physicians, hospital employees, and the general citizenry. Analysis revealed significant and deep support of the Hospital from among its supporters. The Hartsook firm tested a $37 million campaign, a number that was influenced by a previous $10 million campaign that barely made goal and received average gifts in the $15,000 to $20,000 range. Hartsook and Associates recommended a $50 million campaign based on the belief that various departments of the Hospital could make a strong case to the community for support.

"When some first heard of our goal of $50 million, the Board considered it a stretch. But with the results we'd seen in the Hartsook study, we had good reason to believe it was an attainable goal," says Schultz. "We knew the marketplace was shifting, but I think we all enjoy a challenge. When I first saw the numbers, I was reminded of Robert Browning's poem which reflects 'ah, but one's reach should exceed one's grasp'."

There were weeks of review and thought by staff and Board members. Hartsook and Associates proposed a planning period of six months in which to organize the campaign, develop a private campaign and commence solicitation of major gifts. The Foundation used the six months wisely to educate the medical staff, Foundation and Hospital Boards, and put everyone in a "campaign mindset". Board solicitation was purposefully delayed in order to give them confidence in the campaign.

The campaign was quietly initiated in late 1994. Early in the campaign the Wall Street Journal published an article indicating that Columbia Health Care System was interested in acquiring Saint Luke's. While the Hospital denied interest in such a purchase, rumors were rampant about the possible elimination of Saint Luke's as a nonprofit hospital. Hartsook and Associates recommended a private campaign that would not necessarily ever go public, to alleviate the fears of how this campaign would be perceived by the community. Ultimately, late in the campaign, a virtual merger occurred with another smaller local hospital. The campaign went public in May, 1997, in the final six months of the campaign.

First Donors Set the Standard

To the surprise of many bystanders, the first gifts were close to home. The initial donor, a doctor, made a gift of $1.2 million. Another co-chair made a gift of $1 million and another, a gift of $500,000. The Boards of Directors of the Hospital and Foundation eventually gave $10 million, with an average gift of more than $100,000 — six times more than in previous campaigns.

A Decentralized Campaign Approach

Hartsook and Associates recommended a unique arrangement in developing liaisons between the Foundation and the various departments of the Hospital, implementing a committee structure that allowed significant involvement by the Board and volunteers. Largely due to this arrangement, 180 Saint Luke's physicians gave $7 million, with an average gift of nearly $100,000.

"One of the most important things I learned in this campaign is that, in healthcare specifically, people give more to the parts than the whole," says Schultz. "Ours was a very de-centralized campaign. In addition to the ordinary major gift apparatus, we had 14 mini-campaigns being conducted, each with its own case statement, list of goals and projects," explains Schultz. "Each project was chaired by a doctor and lay person within that area. Thus, they were able to focus on their own patients and medical staff. When a doctor made a gift, he was giving to his own department. Each individual effort combined to make a system of giving whereby the greatest needs could be met individually within each department."

Challenge Gifts

A unique opportunity came when it was learned, after beginning the campaign, that the State of Missouri allowed a match on gifts that were made for endowed chairs to affiliated institutions. For each endowed chair, the State would match the amount, dollar for dollar. Saint Luke's was successful in endowing six chairs and one professorship in cooperation with the University of Missouri Kansas City School of Medicine. Each chair provides funding to attract a distinguished medical scholar in the fields of neuroscience, internal medicine, cardiovascular research, anesthesiology research, emergency medicine, and metabolism and vascular-disease research. This was especially helpful because the campaign did not receive support from the traditional Kansas City foundations. Further, it was at a time when many corporations were deciding not to give to health care.

Against odds many refused to bet on, the campaign competed with some of the largest campaigns in the history of Kansas City including Science City at Union Station at $250 million; the Nelson Atkins Museum of Art at $150 million; and the Kansas City Royals underwriting campaign of $60 million.

100 Gifts Over $100,000

"We had no 'ultimate' or 'mega gift' compared to the single $25 million gift made to Children's Mercy Hospital, a very successful local children's hospital. Yet, you have to consider, we had never had a single million-dollar gift in any previous campaign," says Schultz. "At the close of the Strength Amidst Change campaign we ended up with 17 million-dollar gifts." The largest individual gift was $2.9 million.

With the assistance of Hartsook and associates, the Foundation developed creative gift packaging for both outright and deferred gifts, as well as life income arrangements. The campaign received 100 gifts of $100,000 or more, and 17 gifts of $1 million or more. Additionally, they were able to build the Heritage Society, the foundation's deferred-gift club, to almost double its level prior to the campaign.

Staff Changes and Volunteer Leadership

A major obstacle the Foundation faced during the campaign was turnover of personnel, including: changes in the presidency of the Hospital, three members of the nine-person Foundation staff went on extended maternity leave, and three staff members left the Foundation. In spite of these obstacles, momentum for the campaign kept a running pace and the cost of the campaign was negligible.

Outstanding leadership was key in propelling the campaign forward. Campaign leadership set the stage leading not only with their words, but with their individual gifts. The campaign was chaired by J. Thomas Burcham and co-chaired by Albert C. Bean, Jr. and Gerald F. Tuohy, MD. Mrs. Aileen Calloway, Board Trustee and a Committee Chair, also provided active leadership during the campaign.

"The success of this campaign really demonstrates the depth of community support for Saint Luke's Hospital and its employees," says Burcham.

A Project Well Done

At project completion, December 31, 1997, the Strength Amidst Change campaign had raised $59 million, surpassing its goal by $9 million. The final breakdown of gifts included $38.5 million outright and $20.5 million in deferred giving, (discounting the deferred gifts' present value) making it the largest Hospital endowment campaign in Kansas City.

More than 2,000 members of the Kansas City community contributed to the campaign, which resulted in 50 major projects and programs, as well as numerous other initiatives. Perhaps the most astounding feature of the campaign is that it produced a face value of $64 million with no national foundation support. Assets are now approaching $100 million, making it one of the largest private teaching hospital endowments in the country.

Recognition was an important part of the campaign, with all items of recognition being personally delivered. The campaign committee worked hard to keep staff members, board members and a roster of more than 2,000 donors informed throughout the campaign. In addition, special recognition banquets were held for all donors.

While "going over goal" is a significant accomplishment for any hospital in today's fund-raising climate, Schultz is quick to point out that it's not the money, but the means to make good things happen that is most significant about the Strength Amidst Change campaign. "We have 50 direct medical benefits and a long-lasting research benefit. This campaign has made philanthropy a much more active ally and displayed a reservoir of good will towards the Hospital," says Schultz. "We are no longer at the whims of what a national 'crisis in healthcare' may dictate. That's the true legacy of the campaign."

What We Learned

St. Luke's campaign highlights many important gift-closing lessons.

1. *A single gift from the right person can set the standard for others.* The physician's gift of $1.2 million was an important signal to other physicians of the expected size of gifts.

2. *Creativity in allowing donors to set their pace and timing to satisfy pledge commitments (within reason) allowed donors to go to higher levels.*

3. *Recognize the role of outside influence, but be true to who you are as an institution.* Donors respect that.

Campaign for Dignity
Cerebral Palsy Research Foundation

When the leadership of the Cerebral Palsy Research Foundation of Kansas (CPRF) embarked on a $10 million endowment campaign, no one could have predicted the dynamic success the "Campaign for Dignity" would encounter. What began as a modest annual fund and endowment effort evolved into a concisely executed Integrated Campaign™ with a $25 million goal, becoming one of the largest campaigns ever conducted for a social-service nonprofit in Kansas.

CPRF is a combination of three significant entities: Center Industries, a nationally recognized program which provides a high-tech business environment offering employment opportunities for people with disabilities; The Timbers, a residential facility for people with disabilities; and the Carney Center for Rehabilitation Engineering, which modifies home and work sites for people with disabilities, as well as conducting one of only two wheelchair seating clinics in Kansas. CPRF's Human Services Division also provides one of the nation's few community-based programs for survivors of traumatic brain injury.

While CPRF had experienced success in attracting and retaining public funding over the years, no formal structure existed for raising funds from the private sector. One of the reasons for this was the organization's strong commitment to the dignity of people with severe physical disabilities. CPRF'S President and Founder, Jack Jonas, wanted assurance that whoever represented them must not subscribe to the "white cane" approach when presenting their case for support to potential philanthropic investors. Several members of CPRF's Board of Directors knew of and respected the work of Hartsook and Associates. The firm was retained to provide an audit for CPRF's annual fund activities, prepare for anticipated estate and planned gifts, as well as conduct an endowment campaign.

CPRF'S leadership requested on-site consulting services for three years. Norma R. Lee, then a senior consultant at Hartsook and Associates, was recruited for the position. The first year's goal was to establish an Annual Giving Program which could generate a minimum of $100,000 in ongoing support. "To accomplish this goal, we named Norma Lee vice president of development," explained Jonas. Within five years, the Annual Fund Program was averaging $250,000 a year. "Hartsook and Associates' Integrated Campaign™ has been critical to our success," said Jonas.

The Integrated Campaign™ concept was developed by Hartsook and Associates to address all revenue streams of an organization. "We were seeing significant fluctuations in giving to Annual Fund activities while capital campaigns were in progress. Adding endowment fund objectives without coordination also caused confusion on the part of the donor," said Lee. "The integrated concept focuses on how each component works together and compliments one another to increase giving at all levels. CPRF was a particularly challenging client because it had pressures to dramatically increase all types of gifts."

While working with the Board of Directors to identify leadership for the newly formed Annual Fund Advisory Council, CPRF began developing the Case for Support for a $10 million endowment campaign. During the pre-campaign assessment process, however, capital improvements to existing facilities, as well as other capital needs were identified and the recommendation was made to set a goal of $25 million.

Taking an organization from a $10 million goal to a $25 million goal at first glance easily appears a miraculous feat in itself. However, CPRF was in a uniquely favorable position to be able to meet several essential criteria set by Hartsook and Associates.

First, and foremost, the integrity and reputation of CPRF was very high. Second, its services were much appreciated and valued by clients. Third, CPRF'S Board consists of successful entrepreneurs capable of influencing a campaign's outcome and who thrive on the challenge of reaching goals. "In some respects, the first confidence builder we encountered during the campaign was to have this group all serving on CPRF'S Board during this watershed moment in the organization's history," explains Norma Lee. "Additionally, during the pre-campaign assessment, an anonymous donor made a substantial deferred gift to the endowment."

The pre-campaign assessment verified that CPRF, while not well known in the philanthropic community, could, with the right volunteer leadership, go forward with a $25 million campaign. The campaign became a strategy to raise $7 million in capital funds for construction and renovation; $16 million in endowment funds through both outright and deferred gifts; and $2 million in program funds through a combination of program grants and a larger annual fund.

Confidence was heightened when Daniel M. Carney, Chairman of the Board of Directors for CPRF and Co-Founder of Pizza Hut, and Daniel J. Taylor, CEO of Property Management, agreed to co-chair the campaign. Both of these men are major philanthropic investors in CPRF and share an unwavering commitment to the organization's mission.

"CPRF is an excellent organization that has provided support for people with disabilities for many years," says Dan Carney. "Our problem has always been our ability to raise financial support from our community. We were excited to see the plans that were put in place that resulted in our anticipated success."

Carney and Taylor recruited outstanding community leaders to serve with them on the Steering Committee.

The old fund-raising adage that campaigns succeed or fail based on the strength and commitment of the volunteer leadership was certainly underscored throughout CPRF'S two-year Campaign for Dignity. Good staff support was also crucial to the success of the campaign.

"The management and correct utilization of volunteers' time is crucial to the outcome of a campaign. Each volunteer has a particular strength," says Lee. "It is the staff's responsibility to know these strengths and when to call upon them in much the same way a successful coach knows which players need to be in position during a crucial time of a championship game."

CPRF's Case Statement outlined the need to expand the Daniel M. Carney Rehabilitation Engineering Center; renovate The Timbers, a 100-unit apartment complex designed for people with physical disabilities; build a new 14,000-square-foot facility to relocate several of CPRF'S programs; acquire new equipment for Center Industries Corporation, the manufacturing division of CPRF where 75% of the production work force have physical disabilities; and program support.

Through a series of personal presentations, the Campaign for Dignity secured over 75% of the campaign goal the first year. This included two major challenge grants — one from The J. E. and L. E. Mabee Foundation in Tulsa, Oklahoma for $1.5 million and another from The Kresge Foundation in Troy, Michigan for $600,000. The challenge grant from The Kresge Foundation remains the largest awarded to a Kansas organization.

Both challenge grants were awarded on the campaign needs outlined in the Case Statement. Then, a miracle occurred.

CPRF was within a month of satisfying The Mabee Foundation challenge and within three months of meeting The Kresge Foundation challenge when board member and campaign co-chair Dan Taylor successfully negotiated the purchase of a 36,000-square-foot former psychiatric hospital which was adjacent to CPRF'S campus and in almost mint condition.

Very quickly, CPRF'S leadership wrote to both Foundations outlining the advantages to renovating an existing facility as compared to constructing a new one. "The renovation actually cost less per square foot than the cost would be for the construction of a new facility and the additional space would enable CPRF to relocate programs and services, now scattered both on and off its campus, into one central location," recalls Lee. "This would create greater efficiency in the delivery of services and the building provided CPRF a presence on 21st Street, which is a main street in northeast Wichita."

So perfectly did this building match the needs of CPRF, it became known throughout the rest of the campaign as the "Miracle on 21st Street." To their credit, both The Mabee Foundation and The Kresge Foundation agreed to this change in plans and today, the Daniel J. Taylor Administrative Center exists as a reminder that even today, miracles can still happen.

Yet, miracles alone weren't responsible for CPRF's dynamic success. It took hard work, commitment to the organization and its goals, and a well-structured, integrated approach to fund raising to raise a groundbreaking $25 million — funds that will continue to preserve the dignity of those with disabilities through outstanding services for many years to come.

What We Learned

CPRF provides several key lessons to closing a gift.

1. *Integrity and reputation do matter.* Even though CPRF had not been soliciting private gifts — they were respected.

2. *Former board members who may appear not to have significant wealth may make very large gifts.*

3. *Integration.* Seek to solicit your donors from a variety of strategies — estate gifts, outright gifts, in-kind gifts, etc.

(This article was written by Christine Wheat, in consultation with Dr. Robert F. Hartsook.)

About the Author

Bob Hartsook as an author, speaker and consultant, has influenced the direction of philanthropy. His thoughts and experiences have helped both the novice and the experienced fund raiser in closing significant gifts. Speaking to thousands of professionals and volunteers, he focuses on the demands of raising funds today. His trademarked Integrated Fund-Raising Campaign has helped countless institutions achieve maximum financial goals. On the pages of the most popular fund-raising journals, magazines and newsletters, including *Fund Raising Management, NSFRE News, Chronicle of Philanthropy, Planned Giving Today, NonProfit Times* and many others, he articulates the significant challenges facing fund raisers. *Closing that Gift!* was Dr. Hartsook's first book. It was followed by *How to Get Million Dollar Gifts and Have Donors Thank You.*

Prior to starting Hartsook and Associates in 1987, Dr. Hartsook served as Executive Vice President of the Kansas Engineering Society and Vice President of Colby Community College, Washburn University and Wichita State University. At Wichita State he was named president of the Board of Trustees. His consulting firms, Hartsook and Associates and Essential Philanthropic Services, have conducted hundreds of campaigns and regularly maintain a diverse national client list.

Dr. Hartsook holds a Bachelor of Arts in Economics, a Master of Science in Counseling, a Juris Doctor and a Doctor of Education Degree. His lives with his son, Austin, in Wilmington, North Carolina.

Dr. Robert F. Hartsook, President
Hartsook and Associates
1501 Castle Rock
Wichita, KS 67230
Telephone: 316.733.7100
Facsimile: 316.733.7103
E-mail: info@hartsookgroup.com
website: hartsookgroup.com

ASR Philanthropic Publishing

ASR Philanthropic Publishing serves the fund-raising and philanthropic community with a wide variety of publications designed to inform and educate, and to stimulate thought and discussion by professionals throughout the United States.

ASR publications include newsletters, books and monographs, as well as audio and video products.

ASR's Reference Collection monographs and books may be purchased in small or large quantities. Discounts apply to large-quantity orders.

For large-quantity monograph orders, ASR can imprint your organization's logo or trademark on each copy.

ASR also can customize and bind collections of monographs that meet your organization's reference needs.

ASR Philanthropic Publishing also has an active custom-publishing division that creates books, newsletters, brochures and other print material for use by fund-raising and philanthropic organizations. We are available to consult on your organization's specific needs.

For information about any of ASR's programs, or to order, please contact:

ASR Philanthropic Publishing
P.O. Box 782648
Wichita, Kansas 67278
Telephone 316.733.7470
Facsimile 316.733.7103
e-mail books@ASRpublishing.com
website: ASRpublishing.com